THE **Christmas Candy** BOOK

THE **Christmas Candy** BOOK

LOU SEIBERT PAPPAS

Photographs by FRANKIE FRANKENY

CHRONICLE BOOKS
SAN FRANCISCO

Library of Congress Cataloging-in-Publication Data:

Pappas, Lou Seibert.
  The Christmas candy book / by Lou Seibert Pappas ; photo-
graphs by Frankie Frankeny.
        p. cm.
Includes index.
  ISBN 0-8118-3643-6
  1. Christmas cookery. 2. Candy. I. Title.
  TX739.2.C45 P348 2002
  641.8'53—dc21
                                    2002001807

Manufactured in China.

Designed and typeset by Anne Galperin.

M&M's ® Brand is a registered trademark of Mars, Inc.

Distributed in Canada by Raincoast Books
9050 Shaughnessy Street
Vancouver, BC V6P 6E5

10 9 8 7 6 5 4 3 2 1

Chronicle Books LLC
85 Second Street
San Francisco, California 94105

www.chroniclebooks.com

acknowledgments

With many thanks for the support of my enthusiastic
confectioners: Bunny Callahan, Catherine Cadloni, Renee
Ann Fills, Helene Fertig-Katzen, Hilda Guzzetta, Cara Lin,
Christopher Lynch, Cynthia Marshall Schuman, Margie
Stapleton, Nancy Tune, Anna West, and Becky Witter.
And a special thanks to Micki Weinberg for her chocolate
expertise.

contents

7   introduction

     9   A SHORT HISTORY OF CHRISTMAS CANDY

     10   INGREDIENTS

     13   EQUIPMENT

     16   TECHNIQUES

     21   PACKAGING CANDIES FOR GIFTS AND MAILING

23   classic christmas candies

41   terrific truffles

57   family favorites

75   fruit & nut confections

     90   SOURCES

     92   INDEX

     96   TABLE OF EQUIVALENTS

Elite Confections, San Francisco, c. 1910

introduction

Fudge parties and taffy pulls were favorite year-round activities while I was growing up in Oregon's Willamette Valley. Later, when I moved to California and began working for a food magazine, I discovered the joys of making lollipops and hard candies, caramels and divinity. Yet it wasn't until my first trip to Europe that I was introduced to the rich and varied world of Christmas confections.

In Tuscany, the nut-filled rounds of cocoa-dusted *panforte* and chewy squares of hazelnut-strewn *torrone* captivated me. In Scandinavia and at the bountiful German Christmas markets, I was enchanted by the marzipan ladybugs, pigs, and fruits. I found that pralines threaded their sweet crunch throughout the Continent, and I devoured the crystalline morsels at every stop.

Back home, I married into a first-generation Greek family in the candy business. In downtown San Francisco, a year before the big 1906 earthquake, my father-in-law had opened Elite Confections, a candy store and ice cream parlor. In the 1920s, he operated a chocolate shop on Long Island, where his three sons worked alongside him, pulling the taffy and cranking the gears that squirted out peppermint-stick candy. Big copper candy tubs were used for cooking fudges, caramels, and a variety of hard candies in a spectrum of flavors—lemon, lime, raspberry, cherry, and coffee. One of his ten-gallon copper candy kettles now stands on my hearth as a firewood holder, and his antique hard-candy molds sit nearby, awaiting a confectioner.

On the dozens of trips abroad that followed my first one, I have visited the world's finest candy shops in France, Belgium, Switzerland, and Germany. In their kitchens, I have watched as master candy makers transformed simple ingredients into elaborate marzipan, chocolate, nougat, and fruit confections for the holiday season. I used what I learned on those journeys to re-create seasonal favorites in my own kitchen.

This Christmas candy book offers the best of those international sweets—*panforte, torrone,* nougat, truffles, toffee, marzipan—alongside such all-American classics as caramel corn, fudge, and vinegar taffy. Some of the candies are easy to fashion, making them ideal for a family holiday project, while others require the precise skill and timing of an accomplished cook.

Candy is a particularly festive way to share the spirit of the season with family, neighbors, and friends. The recipes that follow are divided into four chapters to fit a variety of holiday roles.

The first chapter, "Classic Christmas Candies," comprises recipes that have long been made at holiday time. The second chapter, "Terrific Truffles," presents ten recipes for a beloved chocolate confection that has moved from the candy-shop kitchen to the home kitchen. Easy to make in lots of irresistible flavors, the truffle has become the amateur candy maker's most popular product.

The third chapter, "Family Favorites," delivers a cornucopia of all-American sweets, from fudges, caramels, and turtles to lollipops, taffies, and caramel corn. These are a joy for youngsters of all ages to make. Chocolate-laced candies studded with fresh and dried fruits and nuts make up the final chapter, "Fruit & Nut Confections."

Homemade candies are a special treat at Christmastime. Use this collection of holiday recipes to make seasonal sweets for your own table and for gift giving to family, neighbors, and friends.

A Short History of Christmas Candy

Candies of all types have been part of Christmas festivities for centuries. Sugarplums, dried and candied fruits bound with honey, graced holiday tables in Byzantine times, while nougat, which dates back to the days of the Roman Empire, has long been one of the thirteen desserts served at Christmas Eve celebrations in Provence. Even today's popular honey-and-nut-streaked *panforte* was already a traditional holiday gift in sixteenth-century Tuscany.

The Crusaders brought marzipan back to Italy from the Middle East in the form of coins the Italians called *marchepane*. Colorful, artful marzipan figures soon became part of Christmas celebrations throughout Europe, especially in Germany, and are still popular today.

Around the same time, monks were making a name for their monasteries by fashioning elaborate expressions of sugar cookery, a culinary art that would later move into the kitchens of apothecaries, where certain confections were sold alongside medicines. Italy's famed nougat, *torrone,* was invented in Cremona for the 1441 wedding of Francesco Sforza, the Duke of Milan. Today *torrone,* beautifully packaged, is given as a Christmas gift almost everywhere in Italy.

America saw the invention of the peppermint-stick candy cane. According to legend, in 1670, during the living crèche ceremony in a Massachusetts cathedral, candy canes, said to represent shepherds' crooks, were handed out to keep children quiet or to reward children who had recited their prayers. Not long after, candy canes were used as ornaments on Christmas trees along with edibles such as marzipan figures, and strings loaded with popcorn and cranberries.

In 1744, Marie Antoinette set her *chocolatier* to work developing fancy confections such as chocolate mixed with powdered orchid bits, almond milk, or orange blossoms. Today, these flavorings carry over to the profusion of truffles that appear in confectionery shops in Paris during the holidays. The English have long satisfied their Christmastime sweet tooth with a simpler sweet, nut brittle, one of the oldest and easiest candies to make, now packaged for seasonal gift giving.

In Europe, praline refers to any candy with a coating, while in England and America, it usually describes a nut brittle that is crushed to a powder. But in Louisiana, pralines are round candy wafers made from sugar, butter, and pecans and are enjoyed along with eggnog at Southern holiday parties. In New England, taffy, fudge, and caramels also claim a long history as seasonal treats.

Candy making—and eating—is a much-anticipated part of Christmastime. With this collection of recipes, home candy makers can create their own holiday candy history.

Ingredients

Top-quality ingredients produce the best-tasting candies. You will be disappointed in your candy-making efforts if you use inexpensive chocolate, imitation flavorings, or less-than-fresh nuts. All of the following ingredients are available in specialty-food stores and well-stocked supermarkets.

Butter

Always use unsalted butter. It contains less water and has a fresher flavor than salted butter. It is more perishable than regular butter, however, because salt is a preservative, so plan to refrigerate it for no longer than a week, or freeze it for longer storage. Wrap the butter tightly and avoid placing it next to strong-flavored foods.

Chocolate

After sugar, chocolate is perhaps the most important ingredient in candy making. In some candies, it is the central element, and in others, a coating or an ingredient.

A number of options exist when buying chocolate, from premium bar chocolate by European and American manufacturers to packaged chocolate chips. Buy a premium brand if you can afford it, of course. For ease, convenience, and economy, many cooks prefer good-quality bar chocolate or chocolate chips, both of which were used to test the recipes in this book.

Chocolate comes from the pods of the tropical cacao tree. Each pod yields 20 to 40 beans the size of a Brazil nut. The beans are fermented, dried, roasted, and then cracked to separate the nibs, which contain about 54 percent cocoa butter, from the shells. The nibs are ground to extract cocoa butter and a crumbly chocolate liquor. The final steps involve conching to knead and mix the liquor into a creamy, smooth liquid, and tempering to stabilize it.

Many types of chocolate are sold. Unsweetened, or baking, chocolate is unadulterated chocolate liquor. Dark bittersweet, semisweet, and sweet chocolates are chocolate liquor with the addition of cocoa butter, a small amount of sugar, vanilla, and usually lecithin. Even though milk chocolate has the same base, but with the addition of dry milk powder, it cannot be used interchangeably with the dark chocolates in recipes. White chocolate is composed of cocoa butter, milk solids, and sugar. It is not technically chocolate, as it does not contain chocolate liquor. Couverture, a type of chocolate used by professional confectioners, has a high percentage of cocoa butter, making it ideal for thin, smooth coatings on truffles and other candies. It must be tempered and is available in cookware stores and by mail order.

Unsweetened cocoa powder is available in two different styles: American nonalkalized and Dutch process. In the American powders, the natural acid in the chocolate is untreated, resulting in a robust taste; in European cocoas, the acid is neutralized, giving the cocoa a milder taste but darker color. Use the type you prefer in these recipes.

Cream

Use pasteurized whipping cream, sometimes labeled heavy cream or heavy whipping cream, with a milk fat content of 32 to 36 percent. Avoid ultrapasteurized cream, which has a slightly cooked flavor because of the high temperature to which it is heated to extend its shelf life. Half-and-half, basically half milk and half cream, contains 10 to 18 percent milk fat.

Flavorings

Candies are flavored with brandies and liqueurs, various extracts such as vanilla and almond, instant coffee granules or instant espresso powder, and other flavorings. For hard candies cooked to high temperatures, flavoring oils, such as lemon, orange, anise, and cinnamon, are preferred to extracts because they are less volatile.

Nuts

Many different kinds of nuts—almonds, Brazils, pistachios, walnuts, pecans, peanuts—are used in candy making, for both flavor and texture. Because nuts have a high natural oil content, they become rancid easily, so always store them in the refrigerator for up to 1 month or in the freezer for up to 1 year. For directions on toasting, see page 18.

Oil

Use a flavorless vegetable oil for oiling pans, aluminum foil, marble slabs, and other candy-making surfaces and for adding to chocolate for melting. Store the oil in a cool, dark pantry and use within 3 to 4 months.

Sweeteners

Cane sugar is the most frequently used sweetener in candy making. It foams less than beet sugar, and it comes in many forms. Granulated white sugar, the most common type, is called simply "sugar" in recipes, unless other sugars are also used. Bakers' sugar, which has a consistency that falls midway between granulated sugar and superfine sugar, may be used in its place. Confectioners' sugar, sometimes called powdered sugar, is finely ground granulated sugar with a small amount of cornstarch added to keep it free flowing.

Brown sugar is granulated sugar to which molasses has been added during processing, resulting in a moist, full-flavored product. Light brown sugar has a more delicate, milder flavor than dark brown sugar and is preferred for most of the recipes in this book. Always firmly pack brown sugar for measuring.

Despite the name, the raw sugar sold in the United States is partially refined. Two types of coarse raw sugar, demerara and turbinado, make attractive coatings on candies.

Corn syrup, which is made from cornstarch, is widely used as a sweetener in commercial candy making. It is available in two forms, light and dark, that cannot be used interchangeably. The syrup acts as an interfering agent, preventing sugar from crystallizing and becoming grainy during cooking. Too much corn syrup, however, turns caramels chewy and makes hard candies sticky.

Honey was the world's first sweetener. In candy making, it helps prevent sugar from crystallizing; creates a pleasant, soft texture; and imparts a lovely flavor. Look for 100 percent pure natural honey.

Maple syrup is made by boiling the sap of sugar maple trees until it reduces to a syrup. Use pure maple syrup rather than a blended syrup, which may contain as little as 2 percent real maple syrup.

Equipment

Candy making requires a few top-quality culinary tools, all of which are usually on hand in a well-stocked kitchen. Once you have selected a recipe to make, read all the way through it and then assemble the tools—and the ingredients—you will need before you begin cooking. The recipes in this book do not demand elaborate equipment. The essentials are described here.

Candy Thermometer

A mercury thermometer specifically designed for candy cookery is necessary for many recipes. It measures temperatures from 100° to 400°F. Look for a thermometer with a metal clip for fastening it to the side of a pan, so that the bulb remains suspended in the liquid. Do not allow

the bulb to rest on the bottom of the pan, or the temperature reading will be skewed. Always read the thermometer carefully. Sometimes you may need to wipe off steam to see the numbers clearly. Handle the thermometer with care as well. When you remove it from a hot liquid, place it in hot water to dissolve the sugar coating and then let it cool in the water. Or let it cool on a countertop on a piece of aluminum foil (otherwise, it may adhere to the surface). Never place a thermometer just removed from hot liquid in cold water immediately, or it may break. Also, do not store it in a drawer with other tools that could jostle it about, as the rough treatment may affect its ability to record accurate readings.

Cooling pans

An 8- or 9-inch square metal pan is ideal for cooling caramel, fudge, and nougat. An 8-by-4-inch metal pan is ideal for smaller batches. A 10-by-15-inch metal pan can stand in for a marble slab or board, and baking sheets and a 9-by-13-inch pan are useful for handling bigger candy batches.

Electric mixer and food processor

An electric mixer is necessary for nougat-style candies made with beaten egg whites. A heavy stand mixer is preferred to a handheld mixer, as it frees both hands. A food processor (or blender) is useful for pulverizing praline, mincing dried fruits, and grinding nuts.

Knives

A knife with an 8- or 10-inch tapered blade is ideal for chopping chocolate bars, nuts, and dried fruits. A serrated knife, a heavy chef's knife, or a cleaver is handy for slicing large sheets of candy into pieces.

Marble slab

Because marble maintains a cooler temperature than most other materials and gives off heat quickly, it is an ideal surface on which to turn out candies after cooking. A plastic cutting board or wooden board can be used, but it does not stay as cool or release heat as quickly.

Saucepans

A heavy, 3-quart saucepan will work for most recipes. Copper, cast-iron, enameled cast-iron, anodized aluminum, and stainless steel pans are excellent heat conductors and prevent candy from scorching at high temperatures.

Small tools

For stirring hot mixtures, long-handled wooden spoons with straight-edged bowls are preferred. Since wood does not conduct heat, the utensil will stay cool and will not scratch the pan. Also, sugar crystals do not adhere to wood as readily as they do to metal. Silicon spatulas are good for stirring chocolate, as they do not absorb flavors and do not conduct heat. Flexible metal spatulas in 4- and 6-inch lengths are useful for spreading candy in a pan. An efficient citrus zester, measuring spoons, and measuring cups for both liquid and dry ingredients are essential. A candy or truffle dipper, a long handle with an oval or round bowl at the end, is handy for dipping truffles into chocolate for coating. Without one, a fork will suffice. A 1-inch scoop or a melon baller helps form nice, round candies. When making a sugar syrup, a natural-bristle,

1-inch-wide pastry brush is useful for washing down the sides of the pan to prevent sugar crystals from forming. Household or kitchen scissors are indispensable for cutting taffy and other candies.

Storage containers
Plastic storage containers with airtight lids, or metal tins lined with aluminum foil or waxed paper, are good for storing candy. For holiday gifts, look for charming tins for packing candies.

Techniques

Instructions on two of the most critical aspects of candy making, the proper handling of sugar and sugar syrups and of chocolate, are included here, along with how to toast and skin nuts, how to make nougat, and a few troubleshooting tips.

Chocolate

Always handle chocolate with care, as moisture and heat can destroy it. To melt chocolate, cut or chop it into small pieces and place the pieces in the top pan of a double boiler, using low heat for hot, but not simmering, water. The temperature of the water should not exceed 130° to 140°F for dark chocolate, or 110° to 120°F for white chocolate. Chocolate begins to melt at 80°F and is fully melted at 110° to 115°F for dark chocolate, and slightly lower for white chocolate. Melt it slowly while stirring constantly. Chocolate holds its shape and does not appear to be melted unless it is stirred. Some cooks prefer to use a microwave for melting chocolate, heating it at medium power for 1 minute, then at shorter intervals, stirring well after each interval until smooth. I prefer the double-boiler method, as chocolate can easily overheat in a microwave, causing it to turn grainy or thick or become scorched.

Avoid allowing any steam to get into the chocolate pan as you remove it from the lower pan. A quick wipe of the base should be sufficient. Steam or moisture can cause the chocolate to "seize," or harden. Once this happens, it is difficult to incorporate the chocolate into the candy mixture, and it will not remelt with ease. If your chocolate should seize, add a few drops of vegetable oil and gently remelt, whisking until the chocolate is once again smooth.

The easiest way to chop a block or bar of chocolate is to place it on a cutting board and, using a sharp, heavy chef's knife, cut it into small pieces. To grate chocolate by hand, use the large holes on a metal box grater. If your hands are warm, hold the chocolate with a piece of waxed paper. To grate chocolate in a food processor, fit the processor with the grating disk.

Professional confectioners temper premium chocolate bars, a technique that involves heating, cooling, and then heating chocolate again while stirring constantly. This gives the chocolate a shiny appearance and smooth texture and prevents gray or white streaks, known as

16

"bloom," from forming. All chocolate comes from the factory tempered. Once it is melted, it goes out of temper. Professionals temper any chocolate that will be used for dipping or coating candies.

You can temper chocolate at home by this quick method: Chop 1 pound chocolate into small pieces. Set aside one-third of the chocolate. Put the balance in the top pan of a double boiler and melt over hot water (not to exceed 130° to 140°F), stirring occasionally. Remove the pan from the heat and wipe the base of the top pan dry. Stir in the reserved chocolate in three batches, melting each batch before adding the next one.

Many novice candy makers prefer to work with chocolate chips. They are simple to measure—6 ounces equal about 1 cup—and the addition of a small amount of vegetable oil eases melting and helps to avoid bloom. Several of the recipes in this book call for chocolate chips and this method. The addition of oil to bar chocolate also helps to avoid bloom.

Handling nougat

Nougat is basically sugar syrup aerated by egg whites and then compacted under a weight. Honey and corn syrup lend a chewier texture to the finished product than a plain sugar syrup. Pouring

the hot syrup into the beaten egg whites can be tricky, especially trying to keep the syrup from the sides of the bowl. The best advice is to turn down the mixer speed and to pour the syrup very carefully. When the candy mixture stiffens, add the nuts immediately and turn out the mixture onto a pan lined with edible rice paper (a translucent paper made from the Asian rice-paper plant and available in Asian markets and some supermarkets) or oiled aluminum foil. Top with a second sheet of rice paper or oiled foil, oiled-side down, and then with a baking pan. Place a heavy weight, such as a food can, on the pan and refrigerate the nougat overnight. The next day, remove the weight and pan, and peel away the foil, if used. Slice the nougat into pieces. Wrap the pieces individually in cellophane and store in an air-tight container, or layer the pieces between sheets of waxed paper in the container.

Handling nuts

All kinds of nuts, from almonds and hazelnuts to Brazils and coconuts, are used to add distinctive texture and flavor to candies. Many recipes call for blanched (skinned) almonds or hazelnuts, which is easy to do.

To blanch (remove the skins from) almonds, add a small amount of the nuts to a pan of boiling water and parboil for 2 minutes. Remove from the heat, drain, and let the nuts cool for a few minutes. Then squeeze each nut firmly, popping it from its skin. Spread the nuts on a baking sheet and place in a preheated 325°F oven for 5 minutes to dry. Store in an airtight container.

To blanch hazelnuts, spread the nuts on a baking sheet. Place in a preheated 325°F oven and toast until the nuts color slightly and are fragrant and the skins begin to flake, 10 to 12 minutes. Lay a kitchen towel on a work surface and spill the toasted nuts onto one half of the towel. While the nuts are still warm, fold the uncovered half over the nuts and roll the nuts in the towel with the palms of your hands until the nuts shed their skins. Alternatively, pick up a handful of nuts after they have cooled for 1 or 2 minutes, and rub them between your hands, letting the skins fall free between your fingers. It is difficult to remove every bit of skin from hazelnuts, and it is not essential to do so.

To toast nuts, spread them on a baking sheet and place in a preheated 325°F oven. Toast until the nuts are fragrant and their color deepens slightly, 10 to 12 minutes. Remove from the oven and immediately pour onto a plate to cool.

To chop nuts coarsely, place them on a cutting board and chop with a heavy knife. For ground nuts, place the nuts in a food processor or blender and process, being careful to stop the action while the nuts are still powdery. If you continue beyond this point, the oil in the nuts will be released and the nuts will form a paste. If possible, grind nuts with a small amount of the flour or sugar called for in the recipe you are making.

Sugar and sugar syrups

Preventing the formation of sugar crystals is the aim of every candy cook. The crystals, bits of undissolved sugar, turn a smooth, velvety mixture into a bumpy, grainy one. Some recipes call for corn syrup or molasses as a way to prevent sugaring, but the best solution is careful technique and cooking.

Use a heavy, 3-quart saucepan for most recipes. The pan needs to have a generous capacity to allow for the bubbling expansion of most mixtures during cooking. Off the heat, combine the ingredients and stir together to dissolve the sugar as thoroughly as possible. Place the pan over medium heat. As soon as the syrup begins to boil, cover the pan and let the contents boil for 2 to 3 minutes. Steam will form and wash down the sides of the pan, removing any sugar crystals that may have formed. Uncover and continue boiling, ideally without stirring. Have ready a pastry brush and a bowl of warm water to use if needed to wash down the pan sides, releasing any crystals into the syrup. If the mixture contains milk, butter, or chocolate, or is heated to a temperature of 290°F or more (for brittles and lollipops), stir it occasionally with a wooden spoon to prevent scorching. Stir slowly and do not touch the sides of the pan.

This transformation of sugar and water into syrups and caramel is the basis of many candies. The stage a syrup is allowed to reach, which is defined by temperature, determines the consistency of the syrup once it cools and sets. The less moisture a syrup contains, the harder it will be when it cools.

The temperature for each stage can vary slightly, depending on the addition of other ingredients. Syrups that contain milk or butter will reach each stage at a lower temperature than plain syrups. For this reason, temperatures can differ among recipes. A reliable candy thermometer is the ideal way to test if a sugar syrup has reached the stage indicated in a recipe. In the absence of a thermometer, test the syrup by a dropping a teaspoonful of it into a glass of cold water. The thread stage—fine, soft threads, 1 to 2 inches long—is visible when the syrup is lifted from the pan and when it is dropped into the water. For the other stages, retrieve the spoonful of syrup from the water and press it between your fingers to check for the consistency described in the following chart. Always use a clean, dry spoon to scoop up the syrup from the saucepan.

This chart gives temperature ranges and characteristics for the various stages. If your thermometer is marked at 5°F intervals, you need to check it closely for the correct temperature.

THREAD	223°–234°F	*Forms a fine, soft thread for sugar syrup.*
SOFT BALL	234°–240°F	*Forms a sticky, soft ball for fudge, soft praline.*
FIRM BALL	244°–248°F	*Forms a firm, pliable, sticky ball for caramel.*
HARD BALL	250°–266°F	*Forms a rigid, pliable ball for divinity.*
SOFT CRACK	270°–290°F	*Forms firm, separate strands for taffy, lollipops, toffee.*
HARD CRACK	300°–310°F	*Forms hard, brittle threads that shatter easily for nougat, brittle, toffee.*
CARAMEL	320°–350°F	*Turns transparent and golden to amber for praline, glazes.*

Troubleshooting

If you are making a recipe for fudge or caramel, and the finished candy is under- or overcooked or has sugared, you can save it by recooking it. Put the candy in a heavy saucepan with 1 cup water and place over low heat. Cook, stirring, until blended and the water is absorbed. Increase the heat to medium, bring to a boil, and cook to the appropriate stage on a candy thermometer as indicated in the original recipe. Pour out and cool according to the recipe.

Candies made with beaten egg whites and a sugar syrup, such as divinity, are highly sensitive to moisture in the air. Never make them on a rainy day, and store them in airtight containers. If the stored candies pick up moisture, they can collapse into a pool. Divinity cannot be recooked, but if it still won't hold its shape, place it in a bowl, stir in ¼ cup confectioners' sugar, and let it stand for 10 minutes before spooning into mounds.

If nougat remains soft after beating, put it in the top pan of a double boiler over hot, but not simmering, water and beat constantly until it dries out and becomes firm. Some commercial honeys absorb moisture and make nougat or its Italian counterpart, *torrone,* chewy. The best candy makers in Italy and France use pure natural honey for making their products. To prevent chewy nougat, look for natural honey in specialty-food stores.

Packaging Candies for Gifts and Mailing

Some candies are more perishable than others, so be selective in choosing candies for gift giving. Among those that ship well are *panforte,* brittle, toffee, chocolate bars and bark, fruit confections, and flavored nuts. Fudges, caramels, truffles, and caramel corn are ideal for packaging in a festive manner and hand delivering to friends.

Party-goods shops are an excellent source for such packaging materials as colorful bags, decorative metal tins in graduated sizes, and small, paper candy cups for individual candies. Petite, fluted candy cups in gold foil make handsome containers for packing individual candies, too. They are available 1 inch in diameter and $\frac{5}{8}$ inch deep and are sufficiently sturdy for holding truffles or for soft candies that take the shape of the cup and reveal a fluted design when the cup is peeled away. Small, clear cellophane bags are fun to use because the candies are visible through the wrapper. Some bags are embossed with gold ribbons, while others have holiday motifs. Candies may also be packed in small, clear boxes, in cardboard boxes in interesting shapes—star, hexagon, round, or even a house—or in attractive plastic or glass containers. Place a sheet of waxed paper between the layers of candy packed in a tin or other container.

Small containers are ideal for most candies. For caramel corn, use larger 2-quart containers. Arrange individual candies on a sturdy, flat round or rectangle, wrap in clear cellophane, and then tie with a bright ribbon. For *panforte,* you can give the entire round, leaving it in its baking pan and wrapping the pan in pretty foil, or you can cut the confection into wide wedges, wrap each wedge in foil, and tie the package with a showy ribbon. Enclose chocolate bark in colored cellophane or foil and present it as a whole bar, letting the recipient break it into serving pieces.

If shipping candies, pack them in a plastic container or metal tin and insert the container in a heavy-duty corrugated cardboard box. The box should be larger than the container to allow room for packing materials, such as bubble wrap, popcorn, newspaper, or crumpled paper. Tape the box securely closed, address it clearly, and carry it to your favorite overnight or 2-day mailing service.

christmastime marzipan, page 32

classic christmas candies

PANFORTE OF SIENA | ENGLISH TOFFEE | CHOCOLATE PANFORTE | TORRONE | FRENCH ALMOND NOUGAT | CHRISTMASTIME MARZIPAN | PECAN PRALINES | MACADAMIA CHOCOLATE CRUNCH | PEANUT BRITTLE | HOLIDAY DIVINITY | CHOCOLATE MARZIPAN LOGS

panforte of siena

THE TUSCAN WALLED CITY OF SIENA IS RENOWNED FOR ITS *PANFORTE*, A NUT-AND-SPICE-LACED CONFECTION THAT ORIGINATED IN MEDIEVAL TIMES AND WAS INITIALLY SOLD AT APOTHECARIES AND HERBALISTS. SOMETIMES *PANFORTE* IS DUSTED WITH CONFECTIONERS' SUGAR AND CINNAMON, BUT IT IS MORE STRIKING UNADORNED, THE NUTS FORMING A LOVELY MOSAIC VISIBLE BENEATH THE SHINY HONEY GLAZE.

3 tablespoons all-purpose flour

½ teaspoon ground cinnamon

⅛ teaspoon ground cloves

⅛ teaspoon ground coriander

⅛ teaspoon ground ginger

⅛ teaspoon freshly grated nutmeg

¾ cup chopped candied orange peel

1 cup almonds, toasted (page 18) and coarsely
    chopped

¾ cup hazelnuts, toasted and skinned
    (page 18), then coarsely chopped

½ cup roasted pistachio nuts

1 cup sugar

½ cup honey

2 tablespoons unsalted butter

1 tablespoon water

Preheat the oven to 325°F. Line a 9-inch pie pan or an 8-inch round cake pan with aluminum foil, shiny-side down, extending it up the pan sides. Lightly oil the foil.

In a large bowl, stir together the flour, cinnamon, cloves, coriander, ginger, nutmeg, candied orange peel, almonds, hazelnuts, and pistachios. In a heavy, 3-quart saucepan, combine the sugar, honey, butter, and water and stir to blend. Bring to a rolling boil over medium heat. Boil uncovered for 1 minute, stirring constantly. Remove from the heat and immediately pour the hot sugar mixture over the nut mixture, stirring to coat the nuts. Turn into the prepared pan and, using a flexible metal spatula, spread to form a smooth, even layer.

Bake the *panforte* in the oven until it starts to bubble along the edges and the nuts turn light golden brown, about 20 minutes. Transfer to a rack and let stand in the pan until completely cool, about 1 hour.

When cool, remove the *panforte* from the pan by lifting the edges of the foil and then peeling the foil away. Wrap in aluminum foil and store in a covered container at room temperature for up to 1 week or in the refrigerator for up to 3 weeks. Allow to age for at least 1 day before cutting. To serve, place on a plate with the top facing up to display the nut mosaic, then slice into thin wedges.

MAKES 24 SERVINGS

english toffee

PACKAGE THIS CANDY IN SMALL, CHRISTMAS-THEMED TINS TO KEEP IT CRISP. IT IS AN IDEAL CANDY FOR SHIPPING LONG DISTANCE. OTHER NUTS, SUCH AS PECANS, BRAZILS, OR MACADAMIA NUTS, CAN BE USED IN PLACE OF THE ALMONDS FOR EMBELLISHING THE TOP.

　　1 cup unsalted butter

1¼ cups sugar

　　½ teaspoon baking soda

　　6 ounces bittersweet chocolate, finely chopped, or 6 ounces (about 1 cup) semisweet chocolate chips

　　½ cup finely chopped toasted almonds (page 18)

Line a 10-by-15-inch baking pan with aluminum foil, extending it up the pan sides. Lightly oil the foil.

In a heavy, 3-quart saucepan, combine the butter and sugar. Place over medium-high heat and bring to a boil, stirring constantly. Cover and boil for 2 to 3 minutes. Uncover and insert a candy thermometer in the pan. Continue cooking, stirring occasionally, until the temperature reaches 290°F. If sugar crystals form on the pan sides, wash them down with a pastry brush dipped in warm water. Remove from the heat and immediately stir in the baking soda.

Pour the mixture into the prepared pan. Scatter the chocolate evenly over the top and let stand for a few minutes. The chocolate will melt from the heat of the sugar mixture. Spread the chocolate with a flexible metal spatula to coat smoothly, then sprinkle evenly with the almonds. Refrigerate for 15 minutes to firm up quickly.

Remove from the refrigerator and let cool completely at room temperature until set. Invert the pan onto a work surface, lift off the pan, and then peel off the foil. Break the candy into small chunks. Store in an airtight container at room temperature for up to 1 week or in the refrigerator for up to 1 month.

MAKES ABOUT 3 DOZEN PIECES

chocolate panforte

WHEN DUSTED WITH COCOA POWDER, THIS *PANFORTE* LOOKS LIKE A TEMPTING CAKE. TO GIVE IT A CHRISTMASTIME LOOK, PLACE STAR-SHAPED CUTOUT STENCILS ON TOP AND DUST WITH CONFECTION-ERS' SUGAR SHAKEN THROUGH SIEVE. FOR A REGAL TREAT, SERVE THE PANFORTE WITH PORT.

¼ cup all-purpose flour

3 ounces bittersweet chocolate, grated

¼ cup unsweetened cocoa powder

½ teaspoon ground cinnamon

⅛ teaspoon ground cloves

⅛ teaspoon ground ginger

⅛ teaspoon freshly grated nutmeg

¾ cup chopped candied orange peel

1 tablespoon grated orange zest

2 cups almonds, toasted (page 18) and coarsely chopped

¾ cup firmly packed light brown sugar

⅓ cup honey

2 tablespoons unsalted butter

1 tablespoon water

2 tablespoons unsweetened cocoa powder

Preheat the oven to 325°F. Line a 9-inch pie pan or an 8-inch round cake pan with aluminum foil, shiny-side down, extending it up the pan sides. Lightly oil the foil.

In a large bowl, stir together the flour, chocolate, cocoa, cinnamon, cloves, ginger, nutmeg, candied orange peel, orange zest, and nuts. In a heavy, 3-quart saucepan, combine the brown sugar, honey, butter, and water and stir to blend. Bring to a rolling boil over medium heat. Boil uncovered for 1 minute, stirring constantly. Remove from the heat and imme-diately pour the hot sugar mixture over the chocolate-nut mixture, stirring to coat the nuts. Turn into the prepared pan and, using a flexible metal spatula, spread to form a smooth, even layer.

Bake the *panforte* in the oven until it starts to bubble along the edges, about 20 minutes. Transfer to a rack and let stand in the pan until completely cool, about 1 hour.

When cool, remove the *panforte* from the pan by lifting the edges of the foil and then peeling the foil away. Invert the *panforte* on the rack, so the bot-tom is facing up. Using a fine-mesh sieve, dust the surface lightly with the cocoa powder. Wrap in alu-minum foil and store in a covered container at room temperature for up to 1 week or in the refrigerator for up to 3 weeks. Allow to age for at least 1 day before cutting. To serve, slice into thin wedges.

MAKES 24 SERVINGS

torrone

AMONG THE TRICKIEST OF ALL THE CANDIES TO MAKE, *TORRONE* IS NUGGETED WITH NUTS, RICH WITH HONEY, AND HAS A SLIGHTLY SOFT, TAFFYLIKE SHELL. RECIPES FOR *TORRONE* ARE SCARCE IN COOKBOOKS, POSSIBLY BECAUSE HONEY IS AN EXTREMELY VARIABLE INGREDIENT AND CAN BE TROUBLESOME DUE TO ADULTERANTS IN MANY COMMERCIAL BRANDS. ITALIAN MANUFACTURERS USE NATURAL HONEY TO MAKE *TORRONE*, AND HOME COOKS ARE ADVISED TO DO THE SAME.

$\frac{1}{3}$ cup natural honey

$\frac{1}{3}$ cup light corn syrup

$1\frac{1}{4}$ cups sugar

3 tablespoons water

2 egg whites

$\frac{1}{8}$ teaspoon salt

$\frac{1}{8}$ teaspoon cream of tartar

1 teaspoon almond extract

1 tablespoon grated lemon zest

$1\frac{1}{2}$ cups almonds, toasted (page 18) and coarsely chopped

$\frac{3}{4}$ cup roasted pistachios

Line an 8-inch square baking pan with a sheet of edible rice paper or with aluminum foil, extending it up the pan sides. If using foil, lightly oil it.

In a heavy, 3-quart saucepan, combine the honey, corn syrup, sugar, and water and stir to blend. Place over medium heat, bring to a boil, cover, and boil for 2 to 3 minutes. Uncover and insert a candy thermometer in the pan. Increase the heat to medium-high and cook, stirring occasionally, until the temperature reaches 300°F. If sugar crystals form on the pan sides, wash them down with a pastry brush dipped in warm water.

Meanwhile, using an electric mixer on medium-high speed, beat the egg whites until foamy. Add the salt and cream of tartar, and beat the whites until they hold firm, upright peaks. Reduce the mixer speed to medium and carefully pour the hot syrup into the egg whites, continuing to beat until the mixture cools to room temperature and is very stiff, 8 to 10 minutes. Beat in the almond extract and lemon zest until blended, and then fold in three-fourths each of the almonds and pistachios.

Turn the mixture into the prepared pan and spread evenly with a flexible metal spatula. Scatter the remaining nuts evenly over the top. Lay a second sheet of rice paper or oiled foil, oiled-side down, on top. Place a second pan on top, and then set a heavy object, such as a can of food, on the pan. Refrigerate for 12 hours.

Remove the weight and top pan, and then invert the pan onto a cutting board, lift off the pan, and peel off the foil if used. With a serrated knife, cut the candy into 1-inch pieces, dipping the knife blade in hot water before each cut to rinse away any candy traces. Place individual candies in foil cups, or wrap pieces individually in cellophane or waxed paper. Store in an airtight container at room temperature for up to 3 days or in the refrigerator for up to 3 weeks.

MAKES ABOUT 4 DOZEN PIECES

VARIATION: For *Torrone Nocciola*, substitute $1\frac{1}{2}$ cups hazelnuts, toasted and skinned (page 18), then coarsely chopped, for the almonds, and add $\frac{1}{2}$ cup diced candied orange peel when folding in three-fourths of the nuts.

french almond nougat

A COUSIN TO *TORRONE*, THIS ELEGANT FLUFFY, WHITE CANDY HAS A SLIGHTLY CHEWY TEXTURE.

2 cups sugar

1½ cups light corn syrup

¼ cup water

2 egg whites

⅛ teaspoon salt

⅛ teaspoon cream of tartar

2 teaspoons vanilla extract

½ teaspoon almond extract

2 tablespoons unsalted butter, at room temperature

2 cups almonds or walnuts, toasted (page 18) and coarsely chopped

Line a 9-by-13-inch baking pan with a sheet of edible rice paper or aluminum foil, extending it up the pan sides. Lightly oil the foil.

In a heavy, 3-quart saucepan, combine the sugar, corn syrup, and water and stir to blend. Place over medium heat, bring to a boil, cover, and boil for 2 to 3 minutes. Uncover and insert a candy thermometer in the pan. Increase the heat to medium-high and cook, without stirring, until the temperature reaches 250°F.

Meanwhile, using an electric mixer on medium-high speed, beat the egg whites until foamy. Add the salt and cream of tartar, and beat the whites until they hold firm, upright peaks. Reduce the mixer speed to medium and carefully pour about ½ cup of the hot syrup into the egg whites, continuing to beat until fluffy, 2 to 3 minutes. Return the syrup pan to medium-high heat and cook, stirring occasionally, until it reaches 300°F on the thermometer. Carefully pour the syrup into the beaten egg whites and beat until the mixture cools and stiffens, about 15 minutes. Beat in the vanilla extract, almond extract, and butter. Fold in the nuts.

Turn the mixture into the prepared pan and spread evenly with a metal spatula. Lay a second sheet of oiled foil, oiled-side down, on top. Place a second pan on top, and then set a heavy object, such as a can of food, on the pan. Refrigerate for 12 hours.

Remove the weight and top pan, and then invert the pan onto a cutting board, lift off the pan, and peel off the foil. With a serrated knife, cut the candy into 1-inch pieces, dipping the knife blade in hot water before each cut to rinse away any candy traces. Place individual candies in foil cups, or wrap pieces individually in cellophane or waxed paper. Store in an airtight container at room temperature for up to 5 days or in the refrigerator for up to 3 weeks.

MAKES ABOUT 6 DOZEN PIECES

christmastime marzipan

ALMOND PASTE IS MADE FROM GROUND BLANCHED ALMONDS AND SUGAR. WITH THE ADDITION OF EGG WHITES, A BIT MORE SUGAR, AND A FLAVORING SUCH AS ORANGE-FLOWER WATER, LEMON JUICE, OR ROSE WATER, THE ALMOND PASTE BECOMES MARZIPAN, A POPULAR CONFECTION IN EUROPE AND SOUTH AMERICA. MARZIPAN IS A BIT TEDIOUS TO MAKE, AND BOTH ALMOND PASTE AND MARZIPAN CAN BE PURCHASED IN ROLLS OR CANS.

IN DENMARK, WHERE MARZIPAN IS PARTICULARLY POPULAR, A PINK MARZIPAN PIG IS GIVEN AT CHRISTMASTIME FOR GOOD LUCK. ANOTHER DANISH HOLIDAY CUSTOM CALLS FOR HOSTING AN EVENING MARZIPAN PARTY BEFORE DECEMBER 25. GUESTS ARE SUPPLIED WITH MARZIPAN, DECORATIVE CHOCOLATE SPRINKLES, RAINBOW-HUED SUGAR SPRINKLES, NUTMEATS, COCOA, AND CURRANTS, AS WELL AS PLENTY OF AQUAVIT TO DRINK. EACH PERSON SHAPES AND DECORATES THE MARZIPAN AS DESIRED, AND PRIZES ARE AWARDED FOR THE BEST SCULPTURES.

ALMOND PASTE
   2 cups blanched almonds (page 18)
   2 cups confectioners' sugar, sifted

MARZIPAN
   1 cup almond paste (above)
     About 2 cups confectioners' sugar, sifted
   2 egg whites, beaten until frothy

     Few drops of orange-flower water, fresh lemon
       juice, or rose water

To make the almond paste: Combine the almonds and confectioners' sugar in a food processor and pulse until finely ground. You should have 3 cups.

Use immediately, or wrap in plastic wrap, slip into a resealable plastic bag, and refrigerate for up to 2 months or freeze for up to 6 months. Bring to room temperature before using.

To make the marzipan: In a large bowl or on a work surface, place the almond paste and dust with a few tablespoons of the confectioners' sugar. Using a light touch, make an indentation in the paste and work in the egg whites, flavoring, and the remaining sugar to form a firm dough. You should have about 12 ounces. Use immediately, or wrap in plastic wrap, slip into a resealable plastic bag, and refrigerate for up to 2 months or freeze for up to 6 months. Bring to room temperature before using.

MARZIPAN FRUITS AND VEGETABLES: Decide on which fruits you would like to make, and then color the marzipan with food coloring in an appropriate hue. Shape the marzipan by hand. Place on racks to dry for 1 to 2 hours, and then store in airtight containers in the refrigerator for up to 2 months.

MARZIPAN POTATOES: Roll the marzipan into balls ¾ to 1 inch in diameter, making them slightly irregular. With a chopstick or skewer, prick small holes in the surface of each ball to form "eyes." Roll in sifted unsweetened cocoa powder until evenly coated. Dry and store as for fruits and vegetables (above).

DANISH MARZIPAN PIGS: Color the marzipan pale pink with food coloring. Shape each pig so that it is about 2 inches long. Use cloves or chocolate sprinkles for the eyes. Dry and store as for fruits and vegetables (above).

LÜBECK MARZIPAN HEART: Preheat the oven to 350°F. Place a heart-shaped cookie cutter of any size on a buttered baking sheet. Press the marzipan into the mold, making the marzipan about ⅜ inch thick. Use extra marzipan to form decorations on top, such as leaves or balls. Brush the surface with beaten egg yolk. Bake in the oven until golden brown around the edges, 10 to 12 minutes. Remove from oven and lift off the cookie cutter. To decorate the heart, dip dried cherries and candied orange or lime peel into egg white and place on the warm marzipan. Let cool, then store in an airtight container in the refrigerator for up to 1 month.

pecan pralines

THIS TRADITIONAL SOUTHERN SWEET TANTALIZES WITH CRUNCHY PECANS IN A BROWN SUGAR DISK.
FOR A HOLIDAY PARTY, PILE THESE ON A PEDESTAL CAKE PLATTER FOR A STRIKING PRESENTATION.

1 cup granulated sugar

1 cup firmly packed dark brown sugar

$\frac{1}{2}$ cup half-and-half

$\frac{1}{4}$ cup light corn syrup

1 tablespoon unsalted butter

$\frac{1}{8}$ teaspoon salt

$\frac{1}{2}$ teaspoon maple flavoring

2 cups pecans

Line a baking sheet with waxed paper.

In a heavy, 3-quart saucepan, combine the granulated and brown sugars, half-and-half, corn syrup, butter, and salt and stir until blended. Place over medium heat and bring to a rolling boil. Cover and boil for 2 to 3 minutes. Uncover and insert a candy thermometer in the pan. Increase the heat to medium-high and cook, without stirring, until the mixture reaches 234°F on the candy thermometer. If sugar crystals form on the pan sides, wash them down with a pastry brush dipped in warm water. Remove from the heat and immediately stir in the maple flavoring and pecans. With a wooden spoon, beat the mixture until it thickens and appears granular, about 2 minutes.

Drop the mixture by spoonfuls onto the prepared baking sheet, forming 2-inch rounds. Let cool completely until set. Carefully peel the pralines off the waxed paper. Store in an airtight container between sheets of waxed paper at room temperature for up to 3 days or in the refrigerator for up to 2 weeks.

MAKES ABOUT 3 DOZEN CANDIES

macadamia chocolate crunch

THIS ELEGANT BRITTLE IS GIVEN A HAWAIIAN ACCENT WITH THE ADDITION OF MACADAMIA NUTS. IT IS IDEAL FOR PACKAGING IN A TIN AND THEN SHIPPING IN A CORRUGATED BOX.

1 cup unsalted butter

2 tablespoons water

2 tablespoons light corn syrup

$\frac{1}{8}$ teaspoon salt

1 cup sugar

1 cup coarsely chopped macadamia, cashew, or Brazil nuts, plus $\frac{1}{2}$ cup finely chopped nuts

1 teaspoon vanilla extract

8 ounces bittersweet chocolate, finely chopped, or 8 ounces (about $1\frac{1}{3}$ cups) semisweet chocolate chips

Line a 9-by-13-inch baking pan with aluminum foil, extending it up the sides. Lightly butter the foil.

In a heavy, 2-quart saucepan, melt the butter over medium heat. Add the water, corn syrup, salt, and sugar and stir to blend. Cook, stirring constantly, until the mixture comes to a boil. Cover and boil for 2 to 3 minutes. Uncover and insert a candy thermometer in the pan. Increase the heat to medium-high and cook, stirring occasionally, until the temperature reaches 290°F. If necessary during cooking, wash down the sides of the pan with a pastry brush dipped in warm water to dissolve any sugar crystals.

Add the 1 cup nuts and cook until the temperature reaches 300°F. Remove from the heat and stir in the vanilla extract.

Immediately pour the mixture into the prepared pan and, using a flexible metal spatula, spread it into the corners. Scatter the chocolate evenly over the top and let stand for a few minutes. The chocolate will melt from the heat of the sugar mixture. Spread the chocolate with the spatula to coat smoothly, then sprinkle evenly with the finely chopped nuts. Refrigerate for 15 minutes to firm up quickly.

Remove from the refrigerator and let cool completely at room temperature until set. Invert the pan onto a work surface, lift off the pan, and then peel off the foil. Break the candy into small chunks. Store in an airtight container at room temperature for up to 1 week or in the refrigerator for up to 1 month.

MAKES ABOUT 5 DOZEN PIECES

peanut brittle

IT IS EASY TO VARY THIS BRITTLE BY USING OTHER NUTS, SUCH AS MACADAMIAS OR WALNUTS. FOR A CLASSY HOSTESS GIFT, SLIP THE BRITTLE PIECES INTO A CLEAR CELLOPHANE BAG AND TIE WITH A RIBBON LACED WITH A HOLLY SPRIG.

$1\frac{1}{2}$ cups sugar

$\frac{2}{3}$ cup light corn syrup

$\frac{1}{2}$ cup water

$\frac{1}{4}$ teaspoon salt

$\frac{3}{4}$ teaspoon baking soda

$\frac{1}{2}$ teaspoon vanilla extract

$1\frac{1}{2}$ cups salted roasted peanuts

Lightly oil a large baking sheet.

In a heavy, 3-quart saucepan, combine the sugar, corn syrup, water, and salt and stir to blend. Place over medium heat and bring to a full rolling boil. Cover and boil for 2 to 3 minutes. Uncover and insert a candy thermometer in the pan. Increase the heat to medium-high and cook, stirring occasionally, until the temperature reaches 300°F. If sugar crystals form on the pan sides, wash them down with a pastry brush dipped in warm water. Remove from the heat and immediately stir in the baking soda, vanilla extract, and peanuts. The mixture will bubble and foam.

Pour the mixture onto the prepared baking sheet and spread in a thin layer with a flexible metal spatula. Let cool for 5 minutes, then, with buttered fingertips, stretch the candy as thinly as possible. Let cool completely.

When the brittle is cool, crack into small pieces and store in an airtight container at room temperature for up to 1 week or in the refrigerator for up to 1 month.

MAKES ABOUT $1\frac{1}{4}$ POUNDS

holiday divinity

DRIED CHERRIES AND PISTACHIOS GIVE THESE LIGHT-AS-AIR CANDIES A HOLIDAY LOOK. THEY ARE APPEALING SLIPPED INTO FLUTED PAPER CUPS WITH A HOLIDAY DESIGN IN RED AND GREEN. DO NOT MAKE DIVINITY ON A RAINY OR HUMID DAY, OR THE CANDY WILL BE STICKY.

2 1/2 cups sugar
1/2 cup water
1/2 cup light corn syrup
2 egg whites, at room temperature
1/4 teaspoon cream of tartar
1 teaspoon vanilla extract
1 cup roasted pistachio nuts, chopped
3/4 cup dried cherries, chopped

Line a baking sheet with waxed paper or parchment paper.

In a heavy, 3-quart saucepan, combine the sugar, water, and corn syrup and stir to blend. Place over medium heat and bring to a rolling boil. Cover and boil for 2 to 3 minutes. Uncover and insert a candy thermometer in the pan. Increase the heat to medium-high and cook, without stirring, until the temperature reaches 256°F. If sugar crystals form on the pan sides, wash them down with a pastry brush dipped in warm water.

Meanwhile, using an electric mixer on medium-high speed, beat the egg whites until foamy. Add the cream of tartar, and beat the whites until they hold firm, upright peaks. Reduce the mixer speed to medium and carefully pour the hot syrup into the egg whites, continuing to beat until the mixture cools to room temperature and is very stiff, about 7 minutes. Beat in the vanilla extract until blended, and then fold in the nuts and cherries.

Drop the mixture by 1-inch rounded spoonfuls onto the prepared baking sheet. Let stand until set, about 1 hour. Carefully peel the candies off the paper. Store in an airtight container between sheets of waxed paper at room temperature for up to 3 days or in the refrigerator for up 2 weeks.

MAKES ABOUT 4 DOZEN CANDIES

chocolate marzipan logs

THESE LUSCIOUS CANDIES, IN THE SHAPE OF YULETIDE LOGS, MASQUERADE AS A DELECTABLE DESSERT. MATE THE DECORATIVE GARNISH TO THE LIQUEUR BLENDED INTO THE MARZIPAN FILLING. IF CANDIED ORANGE PEEL IS THE GARNISH, SOAK IT IN A LITTLE GRAND MARNIER OR COINTREAU BEFORE TOPPING THE CHOCOLATE LOGS. FOR A HOLIDAY LUNCH OR DINNER, MARK EACH PLACE SETTING BY PACKAGING THE LOGS IN SMALL CELLOPHANE BAGS OR CLEAR BOXES, EACH HUNG WITH A NAME TAG.

Confectioners' sugar for dusting hands and work surface, plus $\frac{1}{4}$ cup

1 roll (7 ounces) store-bought marzipan, at room temperature

1 tablespoon Grand Marnier or Cointreau, Frangelico, or amaretto

5 ounces bittersweet chocolate, chopped, or 5 ounces (about $\frac{3}{4}$ cup) semisweet chocolate chips

1 teaspoon vegetable oil

16 slivers candied orange peel (page 83); skinned, toasted hazelnuts (page 18); or slivered, blanched almonds (page 18)

Dust a marble slab or chopping board and your hands with confectioners' sugar. Place the marzipan on the work surface and make depressions in it. Knead in the $\frac{1}{4}$ cup sugar and the liqueur. Break off pieces of marzipan about the size of a small walnut. You should have 16 pieces. Roll each piece first into a ball, and then into a log about 2 inches long and $\frac{1}{2}$ inch in diameter.

Line a baking sheet with waxed paper or parchment paper. Melt the chocolate with the oil in the top of a double boiler over hot, not simmering, water, stirring constantly until smooth.

Using a fork, dip a marzipan log into the chocolate, coating completely, and place on the prepared baking sheet. After dipping a few logs, top off each dipped log with the appropriate garnish, using a sliver of orange peel with the Grand Marnier flavoring, a hazelnut with the Frangelico, or a few slivered almonds with the amaretto. Let the chocolate set at room temperature for 1 hour or refrigerate for 15 minutes.

Carefully peel the logs off the paper. Pack in an airtight container between sheets of waxed paper, and store in the refrigerator for up to 2 weeks. Serve at room temperature.

MAKES 16 CANDIES

classic chocolate truffles, page 44

terrific truffles

PEPPERMINT CANDY TRUFFLES | CLASSIC CHOCOLATE TRUFFLES | HAZELNUT PRALINE TRUFFLES | ORANGE LIQUEUR CHOCOLATE TRUFFLES | COGNAC—GOAT CHEESE TRUFFLES | EGGNOG TRUFFLES | PISTACHIO-CHERRY WHITE CHOCOLATE TRUFFLES | RASPBERRY CHOCOLATE TRUFFLES | MOCHA CHOCOLATE TRUFFLES | MACADAMIA-GINGER WHITE CHOCOLATE TRUFFLES

peppermint candy truffles

PEPPERMINT IN THE CANDY AND LIQUEUR LENDS A DOUBLE ELEGANCE TO TRUFFLES THAT ECHO THE CANDY CANES ON THE HOLIDAY TREE.

6 ounces (about 1 cup) white chocolate chips
2 tablespoons whipping cream
2 tablespoons white crème de menthe or peppermint schnapps
6 ounces bittersweet chocolate, chopped, or 6 ounces (about 1 cup) semisweet chocolate chips
1 teaspoon vegetable oil
¼ cup finely chopped peppermint candy cane or peppermint candies

Melt the white chocolate chips with the cream in the top of a double boiler over hot, not simmering, water, stirring constantly until smooth. Remove from the heat and stir in the liqueur. Turn into a small container, cover, and refrigerate until firm, about 2 hours.

Line a baking sheet with waxed paper. Using a 1-inch scoop or melon baller, form the chocolate mixture into balls and drop onto the prepared baking sheet. Place in the freezer until frozen, 1 to 2 hours.

Melt the bittersweet chocolate with the oil in the top of the double boiler over hot, not simmering, water, stirring constantly until smooth. Remove the chocolate balls from the freezer, and line a second baking sheet with waxed paper. Using a fork, turn each frozen chocolate ball in the melted chocolate to coat evenly and transfer to the prepared baking sheet. As every 2 or 3 balls are coated, sprinkle the tops with some of the chopped peppermint candy. If the chocolate cools too much, reheat it and continue coating the balls.

Refrigerate until firm, about 15 minutes, before serving. To keep, store in an airtight container in the refrigerator for up to 1 month or in the freezer for up to 3 months.

MAKES 16 TO 18 CANDIES

classic chocolate truffles

THESE COGNAC-SCENTED TRUFFLES RECEIVE A DOUBLE DIP OF CHOCOLATE, FIRST IN COCOA POWDER AND THEN IN A CHOCOLATE CLOAK. PASS THEM ON PRETTY SILVER TRAYS AT A TREE-TRIMMING PARTY, OR HOST A TRUFFLE PARTY, INVITING FRIENDS TO BRING THEIR FAVORITE TRUFFLES TO SHARE IN THE STYLE OF A COOKIE EXCHANGE.

12 ounces bittersweet chocolate, chopped, or 12 ounces (about 2 cups) semisweet chocolate chips

1 tablespoon unsalted butter

⅓ cup whipping cream

2 tablespoons Cognac

2 tablespoons unsweetened cocoa powder

1 teaspoon vegetable oil

Melt 6 ounces of the chocolate with the butter in the top of a double boiler over hot, not simmering, water, stirring constantly until smooth. Remove the top pan and wipe away any moisture from the base. Heat the cream in a small pan over medium heat until it boils, then stir the cream into the chocolate. Mix in the Cognac. Turn the mixture into a small container, cover, and refrigerate until firm, about 2 hours.

Line a baking sheet with waxed paper. Sift the cocoa powder into a small bowl. Using a 1-inch scoop or melon baller, form the chocolate mixture into balls and drop onto the prepared baking sheet. Then roll each chocolate ball in the cocoa powder to coat lightly and return to the baking sheet. Place in the freezer until frozen, 1 to 2 hours.

Melt the remaining 6 ounces chocolate with the oil in the top of a double boiler over hot, not simmering, water, stirring constantly until smooth. Remove the chocolate balls from the freezer, and line a second baking sheet with waxed paper. Using a fork, turn each frozen chocolate ball in the melted chocolate to coat evenly and transfer to the prepared baking sheet. If the chocolate cools too much, reheat it and continue coating the balls.

Refrigerate until firm, about 15 minutes, before serving. To keep, store in an airtight container in the refrigerator for up to 1 month or in the freezer for up to 3 months.

MAKES 16 TO 18 CANDIES

hazelnut praline truffles

FRANGELICO AND HAZELNUT PRALINE IMBUE THESE DARK-CHOCOLATE TRUFFLES WITH A NUT-FILLED HARMONY. FOR A PARTY, DISPLAY THEM ON THE SIDEBOARD IN A BIG GOBLET ALONG WITH SEASONED NUTS (PAGE 86) AND CHOCOLATE-DIPPED FRUITS (PAGE 88).

HAZELNUT PRALINE:

- 1 tablespoon sugar
- 1 teaspoon unsalted butter
- ¼ cup hazelnuts, toasted and skinned (page 18)

- 12 ounces bittersweet chocolate, chopped, or 12 ounces (about 2 cups) semisweet chocolate chips
- 1 tablespoon unsalted butter
- ¼ cup whipping cream
- 2 tablespoons Frangelico
- 2 tablespoons unsweetened cocoa powder
- 1 teaspoon vegetable oil

To make the praline: Butter a small sheet of aluminum foil. In a small skillet, combine the sugar and butter over medium-high heat and heat, shaking the pan, until the mixture caramelizes, 3 to 4 minutes. Add the nuts and shake the pan to coat them with the caramel. Turn out onto the prepared foil and let cool. Finely pulverize in a blender or food processor.

To make the truffle centers: Melt the chocolate, butter, and cream in the top of a double boiler over hot, not simmering, water, stirring constantly until smooth. Remove from the heat and stir in the liqueur and half the praline. Turn into a small container, cover, and refrigerate until firm, about 2 hours.

Line a baking sheet with waxed paper. Sift the cocoa powder into a small bowl. Using a 1-inch scoop or melon baller, form the chocolate mixture into balls and drop onto the prepared baking sheet. Then roll each chocolate ball in the cocoa powder to coat lightly and return to the baking sheet. Place in the freezer until frozen, 1 to 2 hours.

Melt the remaining 6 ounces chocolate with the oil in the top of a double boiler over hot, not simmering, water, stirring constantly until smooth. Remove the chocolate balls from the freezer, and line a second baking sheet with waxed paper. Using a fork, turn each frozen chocolate ball in the melted chocolate to coat evenly and transfer to the prepared baking sheet. If the chocolate cools too much, reheat it and continue coating the balls. As every 2 or 3 balls are coated, sprinkle the tops with a little of the remaining praline.

MAKES 16 TO 18 CANDIES

orange liqueur chocolate truffles

FRESH ORANGES HAVE LONG BEEN A TRADITIONAL HOLIDAY STOCKING STUFFER. HERE THE ORANGE FLAVOR IN THE PEEL AND THE LIQUEUR EMBELLISHES A CHOCOLATE TRUFFLE.

6 ounces bittersweet chocolate, chopped, or 6 ounces (about 1 cup) semisweet chocolate chips
1 tablespoon unsalted butter
$\frac{1}{3}$ cup whipping cream
2 tablespoons Grand Marnier or Cointreau
2 tablespoons unsweetened cocoa powder
16 slivers candied orange peel (optional; page 83)

Melt the chocolate with the butter in the top of a double boiler over hot, not simmering, water, stirring constantly until smooth. Remove the top pan and wipe away any moisture from the base. Heat the cream in a small pan over medium heat until it boils, then stir the cream into the chocolate. Mix in the liqueur. Turn into a small container, cover, and refrigerate until firm, about 2 hours.

Line a baking sheet with waxed paper. Sift the cocoa powder into a small bowl. Using a 1-inch scoop or melon baller, form the chocolate mixture into balls and drop onto the prepared baking sheet. Then roll each chocolate ball in the cocoa powder to coat lightly and return to the baking sheet. Top each ball with a sliver of candied orange peel, if desired.

Refrigerate until firm, about 15 minutes, before serving. To keep, store in an airtight container in the refrigerator for up to 1 month or in the freezer for up to 3 months.

MAKES 16 TO 18 CANDIES

terrific truffles

cognac-goat cheese truffles

CHOCOLATE-CHEESECAKE LOVERS FAVOR THIS TRUFFLE, WHICH MELDS THE FLAVORS OF COGNAC, GOAT CHEESE, AND CHOCOLATE IN AN EASY-TO-MAKE, COCOA-DUSTED CANDY. FOR A MORE SUBTLE CHEESE FLAVOR, CHOOSE THE NATURAL CREAM CHEESE.

4 ounces bittersweet chocolate, chopped or
4 ounces (about ⅔ cup) semisweet chocolate chips
¼ pound mild, fresh goat cheese or natural cream cheese, at room temperature
1½ tablespoons confectioners' sugar
2 teaspoons Cognac
3 tablespoons unsweetened cocoa powder

Melt the chocolate in the top of a double boiler over hot, not simmering, water, stirring constantly until smooth. Remove the top pan and wipe away any moisture from the base. Let the chocolate cool slightly.

In a bowl, whisk together the cheese, confectioners' sugar, and Cognac until light and fluffy. Whisk in the melted chocolate until combined. Cover and refrigerate until firm, about 1 hour.

Line a baking sheet with waxed paper. Sift the cocoa powder into a small bowl. Using a 1-inch scoop or melon baller, form the chocolate mixture into balls and drop onto the prepared baking sheet. Then roll each chocolate ball in the cocoa powder to coat lightly and return to the baking sheet.

Refrigerate until firm, about 15 minutes, before serving. Store in an airtight container in the refrigerator for up to 1 week.

MAKES ABOUT 2 DOZEN CANDIES

eggnog truffles

THESE CREAMY, RUM-FILLED CANDIES EVOKE THE POPULAR HOLIDAY DRINK. PAIR THEM WITH THE EQUALLY FESTIVE PEPPERMINT CANDY TRUFFLES (PAGE 42).

6 ounces (about 1 cup) white chocolate chips
2 tablespoons whipping cream
2 tablespoons light or dark rum
$\frac{1}{8}$ teaspoon freshly grated nutmeg
6 ounces bittersweet chocolate, chopped,
    or 6 ounces (about 1 cup) semisweet
    chocolate chips
1 teaspoon vegetable oil
1 ounce white chocolate

Melt the white chocolate chips with the cream in the top of a double boiler over hot, not simmering, water, stirring constantly until smooth. Remove from the heat and stir in the rum and nutmeg. Turn into a small container, cover, and refrigerate until firm, about 2 hours.

Line a baking sheet with waxed paper. Using a 1-inch scoop or melon baller, form the chocolate mixture into balls and drop onto the prepared baking sheet. Place in the freezer until frozen, 1 to 2 hours.

Melt the bittersweet chocolate or semisweet chocolate chips with the oil in the top of the double boiler over hot, not simmering, water, stirring constantly until smooth. Remove the chocolate balls from the freezer, and line a second baking sheet with waxed paper. Using a fork, turn each frozen chocolate ball in the melted chocolate to coat evenly and transfer to the prepared baking sheet. If the chocolate cools too much, reheat it and continue coating the balls.

Melt the 1 ounce white chocolate in a small heat-proof bowl over a pan of hot water. Dip a small flexible metal spatula in the white chocolate and drizzle zigzag lines on top of each truffle.

Refrigerate until firm, about 15 minutes, before serving. To keep, store in an airtight container in the refrigerator for up to 1 month or in the freezer for up to 3 months.

MAKES 16 TO 18 CANDIES

terrific truffles

pistachio-cherry white chocolate truffles

THESE SNOWY TRUFFLES ARE DRESSED UP IN HOLIDAY COLORS. EACH BITE EXUDES A TANTALIZING MOUTHFUL OF CHERRY LIQUEUR.

1½ tablespoons dried cherries, chopped, plus 16 to 18 for garnish
2 tablespoons kirsch
6 ounces (about 1 cup) white chocolate chips
2 tablespoons whipping cream
¼ cup raw pistachios, finely chopped

In a small bowl, combine the chopped cherries and kirsch. Let soak for 1 hour.

Melt the chocolate with the cream in the top of a double boiler over hot, not simmering, water, stirring constantly until smooth. Remove from the heat and stir in the chopped cherries and liqueur. Turn into a small container, cover, and refrigerate until firm, about 2 hours.

Line a baking sheet with waxed paper. Place the pistachios in a small bowl. Using a 1-inch scoop or melon baller, form the chocolate mixture into balls and drop onto the prepared baking sheet. Then roll each chocolate ball in the pistachios to coat lightly and return to the baking sheet. Top each truffle with a dried cherry.

Refrigerate until firm, about 15 minutes, before serving. To keep, store in an airtight container in the refrigerator for up to 1 month or in the freezer for up to 3 months.

MAKES 16 TO 18 CANDIES

raspberry chocolate truffles

OF ALL THE TRUFFLES IN THIS BOOK, THESE ARE MY FAVORITE. RASPBERRIES AND CHOCOLATE ARE THE PERFECT MARRIAGE, AND HERE BOTH BERRY JAM AND FRAMBOISE LIQUEUR PROVIDE THE FLAVOR ACCENT IN THE TRUFFLE CENTERS. THESE ARE DIVINE TO PACKAGE IN A DECORATIVE TIN FOR GIFT GIVING.

12 ounces bittersweet chocolate, chopped, or 12 ounces (about 2 cups) semisweet chocolate chips
1 tablespoon unsalted butter
2 tablespoons whipping cream
2 tablespoons seedless raspberry jam
2 tablespoons Framboise
2 tablespoons unsweetened cocoa powder
1 teaspoon vegetable oil

Melt 6 ounces of the chocolate with the butter, cream, and jam in the top of a double boiler over hot, not simmering, water, stirring constantly until smooth. Remove from the heat and stir in the liqueur. Turn into a small container, cover, and refrigerate until firm, about 2 hours.

Line a baking sheet with waxed paper. Sift the cocoa powder into a small bowl. Using a 1-inch scoop or melon baller, form the chocolate mixture into balls and drop onto the prepared baking sheet. Then roll each chocolate ball in the cocoa powder to coat lightly and return to the baking sheet. Place in the freezer until frozen, about 2 hours.

Melt the remaining 6 ounces chocolate with the oil in the top of the double boiler over hot, not simmering, water, stirring constantly until smooth. Remove the chocolate balls from the freezer, and line a second baking sheet with waxed paper. Using a fork, turn each frozen chocolate ball in the melted chocolate to coat evenly and transfer to the prepared baking sheet. If the chocolate cools too much, reheat it and continue coating the balls.

Refrigerate until firm, about 15 minutes, before serving. To keep, store in an airtight container in the refrigerator for up to 1 month or in the freezer for up to 3 months.

MAKES 16 TO 18 CANDIES

mocha chocolate truffles

AN ALLURING COFFEE OVERTONE PERMEATES THESE MILK CHOCOLATE TRUFFLES, AND THE COFFEE BEAN CANDY GARNISH EXPLODES WITH COFFEE FLAVOR. TRUFFLE LOVERS APPLAUD THIS COMBINATION.

6 ounces (about 1 cup) milk chocolate chips

1 tablespoon unsalted butter

$\frac{1}{4}$ cup whipping cream

2 teaspoons instant coffee granules or instant espresso powder dissolved in 1 tablespoon hot water

2 tablespoons unsweetened cocoa powder

16 to 18 coffee bean candies (optional)

refrigerator for up to 1 month or in the freezer for up to 3 months.

MAKES 16 TO 18 CANDIES

Melt the chocolate with the butter and cream in the top of a double boiler over hot, not simmering, water, stirring constantly until smooth. Remove from the heat and stir in the dissolved coffee. Turn into a small container, cover, and refrigerate until firm, about 2 hours.

Line a baking sheet with waxed paper. Sift the cocoa powder into a small bowl. Using a 1-inch scoop or melon baller, form the chocolate mixture into balls and drop onto the prepared baking sheet. Then roll each chocolate ball in the cocoa powder to coat lightly and return to the baking sheet. Top each ball with a coffee bean candy, if desired.

Refrigerate until firm, about 15 minutes, before serving. To keep, store in an airtight container in the

macadamia-ginger white chocolate truffles

THE SPARK OF CANDIED GINGER IGNITES THESE CREAMY, RICH TRUFFLES WITH A LIVELY, WARM ACCENT. FOR A HOLIDAY TRAY, PARTNER THESE CANDIES WITH A DARK CHOCOLATE TRUFFLE, SUCH AS ORANGE LIQUEUR CHOCOLATE TRUFFLES (PAGE 47), AND ARRANGE ON A PLATE WITH A BACKDROP OF GOLD AND SCARLET MAPLE LEAVES.

6 ounces (about 1 cup) white chocolate chips
2 tablespoons whipping cream
2 tablespoons Cognac
1 tablespoon finely chopped candied ginger, plus 16 to 18 slivers for garnish
$\frac{1}{4}$ cup finely chopped macadamia nuts

Melt the chocolate with the cream in the top of a double boiler over hot, not simmering, water, stirring constantly until smooth. Remove from the heat and stir in the Cognac and chopped candied ginger. Turn into a small container, cover, and refrigerate until firm, about 2 hours.

Line a baking sheet with waxed paper. Place the macadamia nuts in a small bowl. Using a 1-inch scoop or melon baller, form the chocolate mixture into balls and drop onto the prepared baking sheet. Then roll each chocolate ball in the nuts to coat lightly and return to the baking sheet. Top each ball with a sliver of candied ginger.

Refrigerate until firm, about 15 minutes, before serving. To keep, store in an airtight container in the refrigerator for up to 1 month or in the freezer for up to 3 months.

MAKES 16 TO 18 CANDIES

peanut butter fudge, page 59

family favorites

OLD-FASHIONED FUDGE | PEANUT BUTTER FUDGE | CHOCOLATE-COATED PECAN CARAMELS | CAPPUCCINO-WALNUT FUDGE BALLS | MAPLE PECAN CARAMELS | LOLLIPOPS | COFFEE-WALNUT CARAMELS | CHOCOLATE CARAMELS | CARAMEL NUT CORN | PECAN TURTLES | VINEGAR CANDY | HONEY TAFFY

old-fashioned fudge

THIS CANDY IS A LONGTIME FAVORITE AND JUST THE KIND OF INDULGENCE THE WHOLE FAMILY LOVES AT CHRISTMASTIME. ALTHOUGH WALNUTS ARE TRADITIONAL, PECANS OR TOASTED HAZELNUTS ARE WONDERFUL, TOO.

2 cups sugar

¾ cup half-and-half

3 tablespoons light corn syrup

⅛ teaspoon salt

6 ounces bittersweet chocolate, chopped or 6 ounces (about 1 cup) semisweet chocolate chips

2 ounces unsweetened chocolate, chopped

2 tablespoons unsalted butter

1 teaspoon vanilla extract

1 cup coarsely chopped pecans, walnuts, or skinned, toasted hazelnuts (page 18)

Line an 8-inch square baking pan with aluminum foil, extending it up the pan sides. Lightly oil the foil.

In a heavy, 3-quart saucepan, combine the sugar, half-and-half, corn syrup, and salt, stirring to blend. Place over medium heat, bring to a boil, cover, and boil for 2 to 3 minutes. Uncover, remove the pan from the heat, and add the chocolates, stirring until completely melted. Return the pan to the heat and insert a candy thermometer in the pan. Increase the heat to medium-high, and cook, without stirring, until the temperature reaches 238°F. If sugar crystals form on the pan sides, wash them down with a pastry brush dipped in warm water. Remove from the heat and let cool to 110°F.

Using a wooden spoon, beat in the butter and vanilla extract until the fudge begins to lose its sheen and holds it shape on the spoon, about 2 minutes. Quickly mix in the nuts. Turn the fudge into the prepared pan and smooth the surface with a flexible metal spatula. Let cool at room temperature until firm, 1 to 2 hours.

Invert the pan onto a cutting board, lift off the pan, and then peel off the foil. Cut the fudge into 1¼-inch squares. Store in an airtight container in the refrigerator for up to 3 weeks.

MAKES ABOUT 3 DOZEN PIECES

peanut butter fudge

THIS KID-FRIENDLY CANDY DELIGHTS PEANUT-BUTTER LOVERS OF ALL AGES. FOR SOME FAMILIES, MAKING THIS CHOCOLATE-FREE FUDGE IS A HOLIDAY TRADITION.

2/3 cup milk

2 tablespoons light corn syrup

2 tablespoons unsalted butter

Pinch of baking soda

1 cup granulated sugar

1 cup firmly packed light brown sugar

1/2 cup smooth or chunky peanut butter

1 teaspoon vanilla extract

3/4 cup coarsely chopped peanuts (optional)

Line an 8-inch square baking pan with aluminum foil, extending it up the pan sides. Lightly oil the foil.

In a heavy, 3-quart saucepan, combine the milk, corn syrup, butter, baking soda, and sugars and stir to blend. Place over medium heat and bring to a boil, stirring occasionally. Cover and boil for 2 to 3 minutes. Uncover and insert a candy thermometer in the pan. Increase the heat to medium-high and cook, without stirring, until the temperature reaches 234°F, stirring occasionally. If sugar crystals form on the pan sides, wash them down with a pastry brush dipped in warm water. Remove from the heat and let cool to 110°F.

Using a wooden spoon, beat in the peanut butter, vanilla extract, and the nuts, if desired. Continue beating until the mixture begins to lose its sheen and holds it shape on the spoon, about 2 minutes. Turn the fudge into the prepared pan and smooth the surface with a flexible metal spatula. Let cool at room temperature until firm, 1 to 2 hours.

Invert the pan onto a cutting board, lift off the pan, and then peel off the foil. Cut the fudge into 1 1/4-inch squares. Store in an airtight container in the refrigerator for up to 3 weeks.

MAKES ABOUT 3 DOZEN PIECES

family favorites

59

chocolate-coated pecan caramels

THESE QUINTESSENTIAL CARAMELS WEAR A SLEEK CHOCOLATE CLOAK. PUT THEM OUT FOR GUESTS AT A HOLIDAY AFTERNOON COFFEE GET-TOGETHER.

2 cups sugar

1 cup whipping cream

¾ cup sweetened condensed milk

1 cup light corn syrup

½ cup unsalted butter

1 teaspoon vanilla extract

1 cup coarsely chopped pecans or walnuts

6 ounces bittersweet chocolate, chopped, or 6 ounces (about 1 cup) semisweet chocolate chips

Line a 9-inch square pan with aluminum foil, extending it up the sides, and lightly oil the foil.

In a heavy, 3-quart saucepan, combine the sugar, cream, milk, corn syrup, and butter and stir to blend. Place over medium heat and bring to a boil, stirring occasionally. Cover and boil for 2 to 3 minutes. Uncover and insert a candy thermometer in the pan. Increase the heat to medium-high and cook, stirring occasionally, until the temperature reaches 246°F. If sugar crystals form on the pan sides, wash them down with a pastry brush dipped in warm water.

Remove from the heat and stir in the vanilla extract and nuts. Turn into the prepared pan and spread with a flexible metal or silicon spatula. Scatter the chocolate evenly over the hot candy and let stand for a few minutes until it melts. Spread the chocolate with the spatula to coat smoothly. Refrigerate until firm, 1 to 2 hours.

Invert the pan onto an oiled cutting board, lift off the pan, and peel off the foil. Using a sharp knife, cut into 1-inch squares. Store in an airtight container between sheets of waxed paper or individually wrapped in waxed-paper squares. The caramels will keep at room temperature for 3 days, in the refrigerator for up to 2 weeks, or in the freezer for up to 1 month.

MAKES 64 CANDIES

cappuccino-walnut fudge balls

THIS CANDY BRINGS TOGETHER THE FLAVORS OF THE POPULAR COFFEE DRINK. THE MIXTURE IS SLIGHTLY SOFT AND CREAMY, MAKING IT EASY TO ROLL INTO BALLS AND TAKE ON A CHOPPED-NUT COATING.

2 cups sugar

1 cup half-and-half

2 tablespoons instant coffee granules or instant espresso powder dissolved in $\frac{1}{4}$ cup hot water

2 tablespoons corn syrup

2 tablespoons unsalted butter

$\frac{1}{8}$ teaspoon salt

1 teaspoon vanilla extract

1 cup finely chopped walnuts or pecans

Line a baking sheet with waxed paper.

In a heavy, 3-quart saucepan, combine the sugar, half-and-half, dissolved coffee, corn syrup, butter, and salt and stir to blend. Place over medium heat and bring to a boil, stirring occasionally. Cover and boil for 2 to 3 minutes. Uncover and insert a candy thermometer in the pan. Increase the heat to medium-high and cook, stirring occasionally, until the temperature reaches 238°F. If sugar crystals form on the pan sides, wash them down with a pastry brush dipped in warm water. Remove from the heat, stir in the vanilla, and let cool to 110°F.

Using a wooden spoon, beat until the fudge begins to lose its sheen and holds it shape on the spoon, about 2 minutes. Chill until cool, about 30 minutes. Form into 1-inch balls and place on the prepared baking sheet. Place the nuts in a small bowl, and roll the balls in the nuts to coat lightly. Return them to the baking sheet.

Refrigerate until firm, about 30 minutes, before serving. Store in an airtight container in the refrigerator for up to 2 weeks.

MAKES ABOUT 3 DOZEN CANDIES

maple pecan caramels

PURE MAPLE SYRUP LENDS A DELICIOUS FLAVOR AND AROMA TO THESE CARAMELS. EVEN THOUGH SUGARING TIME COMES AFTER THE HOLIDAYS, NEW ENGLAND COOKS ALWAYS HAVE SOME SYRUP ON HANDY FOR TURNING OUT THESE HOLIDAY CANDIES.

1 cup firmly packed light brown sugar

$\frac{1}{2}$ cup whipping cream

$\frac{1}{4}$ cup milk

$\frac{1}{2}$ cup maple syrup

2 tablespoons unsalted butter

$\frac{1}{2}$ teaspoon vanilla extract

$\frac{1}{2}$ cup coarsely chopped toasted pecans or
    walnuts (page 18)

Line an 8-by-4-inch baking pan with aluminum foil, extending it up the sides. Lightly oil the foil.

In a heavy, $2\frac{1}{2}$-quart saucepan, combine the brown sugar, cream, milk, maple syrup, and butter and stir to blend. Place over medium heat and bring to a boil, stirring occasionally. Cover and boil for 2 to 3 minutes. Uncover and insert a candy thermometer in the pan. Increase the heat to medium-high and cook, stirring occasionally, until the temperature reaches 246°F. If sugar crystals form on the pan sides, wash them down with a pastry brush dipped in warm water. Remove from the heat and stir in the vanilla extract and nuts.

Turn the mixture into the prepared pan and spread with a flexible metal or silicon spatula. Refrigerate until firm, 1 to 2 hours.

Invert the pan onto an oiled cutting board, lift off the pan, and then peel off the foil. Using a sharp knife, cut into 1-inch squares. Store in an airtight container between sheets of waxed paper or individually wrapped in waxed-paper squares. The caramels will keep at room temperature for up to 3 days, in the refrigerator for up to 2 weeks, or in the freezer for up to 2 months.

MAKES ABOUT 2 DOZEN CANDIES

lollipops

THESE OLD-FASHIONED CANDIES ARE A WONDERFUL CHRISTMAS TREAT FOR YOUNGSTERS. THEY ALSO LOOK CHARMING DECORATING A HOLIDAY TREE: USE CELLOPHANE-WRAPPED LOLLIPOPS TO DECK THE BOUGHS OF A SMALL EVERGREEN DISPLAYED ON A TABLETOP.

YOU CAN USE CONCENTRATED FOOD COLORING AND FLAVORING IN THE SYRUP, BUT FOR THE FRESH-EST FLAVOR, MAKE THE SYRUP WITH FRUIT JUICE. RASPBERRIES, BLUEBERRIES, BLACKBERRIES, GRAPES, AND PINEAPPLE ARE ALL SUITABLE FOR FLAVORING LOLLIPOPS. GENTLY HEAT THE FRUIT UNTIL THE JUICE BEGINS TO FLOW, THEN STRAIN THROUGH A JELLY BAG. SUBSTITUTE $\frac{1}{3}$ CUP STRAINED FRUIT JUICE FOR THE WATER, AND OMIT THE FLAVORING AND COLORING.

1 cup sugar

$\frac{1}{3}$ cup light corn syrup

$\frac{1}{3}$ cup water

1 or 2 drops oil of anise, cinnamon, clove, lemon, or orange

Few drops of red, yellow, blue, or green food coloring

Oil a marble slab or a baking sheet. Have ready at least a dozen wooden sucker sticks.

In a heavy, 2-quart saucepan, combine the sugar, corn syrup, and water and stir to blend. Place over medium heat and bring to a boil, stirring occasionally. Cover and boil for 2 to 3 minutes. Uncover and insert a candy thermometer in the pan. Increase the heat to medium-high and cook, stirring occasionally, until the temperature reaches 290°F. If sugar crystals form on the pan sides, wash them down with a pastry brush dipped in warm water. Remove the pan from the heat and immediately dip the bottom of it into a pan of cold water to arrest the cooking. Add the flavoring and coloring of choice. Let cool to 280°F.

Using a large metal spoon, immediately spoon 1½-inch pools of syrup onto the prepared marble slab. Lay one end of the lollipop stick in each pool of syrup while it is still soft and push gently to secure in place. Dot a little extra syrup on the embedded end of the stick. Let cool at room temperature until completely set, about 2 hours.

Wrap each lollipop in cellophane or waxed paper. Store in an airtight container at room temperature for up to 1 month.

MAKES ABOUT 12 CANDIES

coffee-walnut caramels

ESPRESSO POWDER LENDS A RICH FLAVOR TO THESE CARAMELS. GIFT WRAP THEM ALONG WITH A PACKAGE OF PREMIUM COFFEE BEANS TO DELIGHT A COFFEE-LOVING FRIEND.

$\frac{1}{2}$ cup granulated sugar

$\frac{1}{2}$ cup firmly packed dark brown sugar

$\frac{1}{2}$ cup whipping cream

$\frac{1}{4}$ cup milk

$\frac{1}{3}$ cup light corn syrup

2 tablespoons honey

1 tablespoon unsalted butter

$\frac{1}{2}$ cup walnuts or pecans, toasted (page 18) and coarsely chopped

1 tablespoon instant coffee granules or instant espresso powder dissolved in 2 teaspoons hot water

Line an 8-by-4-inch pan with aluminum foil, extending it up the sides, and lightly oil the foil.

In a heavy, $2\frac{1}{2}$-quart saucepan, combine the sugars, cream, milk, corn syrup, honey, and butter, stirring to blend. Place over medium heat and bring to a boil, stirring occasionally. Cover and boil for 2 to 3 minutes. Uncover and insert a candy thermometer in the pan. Increase the heat to medium-high and cook, stirring occasionally, until the temperature reaches 246°F. If sugar crystals form on the pan sides, brush them down with a pastry brush dipped in warm water. Remove from the heat and stir in the nuts and dissolved coffee.

Turn the mixture into the prepared pan and spread with a flexible metal or silicon spatula. Refrigerate until firm, 1 to 2 hours.

Invert the pan onto an oiled cutting board, lift off the pan, and then peel off the foil. Using a sharp knife, cut into 1-inch squares. Store in an airtight container between sheets of waxed paper or individually wrapped in waxed-paper squares. The caramels will keep at room temperature for up to 3 days, in the refrigerator for up to 2 weeks, or in the freezer for up to 2 months.

MAKES ABOUT 2 DOZEN CANDIES

chocolate caramels

THESE LUSCIOUS, CHEWY CANDIES HAVE A SMOOTH CHOCOLATE FLAVOR AND A DELIGHTFUL CRUNCH OF NUTS. PREPARE A DOUBLE BATCH IF YOU WANT THEM FOR GIFT GIVING. THEY KEEP WELL IN THE FREEZER, SO YOU CAN MAKE THEM AHEAD OF THE HOLIDAY RUSH.

1 cup firmly packed light brown sugar
$\frac{1}{4}$ cup natural honey
$\frac{1}{2}$ cup milk
2 ounces unsweetened chocolate, chopped
1 tablespoon unsalted butter
$\frac{1}{2}$ teaspoon vanilla extract
$\frac{1}{2}$ cup coarsely chopped toasted pecans or walnuts (optional; page 18)

Line an 8-by-4-inch pan with foil, extending it up the sides. Lightly oil the foil.

In a heavy, $2\frac{1}{2}$-quart saucepan, combine the brown sugar, honey, milk, and chocolate and stir to blend. Place over medium heat and bring to a boil, stirring occasionally. Cover and boil for 2 to 3 minutes. Uncover and insert a candy thermometer in the pan. Increase the heat to medium-high and cook, stirring occasionally, until the temperature reaches 255°F. If sugar crystals form on the pan sides, wash them down with a pastry brush dipped in warm water. Remove from the heat and stir in the butter, vanilla extract, and the nuts, if desired.

Turn the mixture into the prepared pan and spread with a flexible metal or silicon spatula. Refrigerate until firm, 1 to 2 hours.

Invert the pan onto an oiled cutting board, lift off the pan, and then peel off the foil. Using a sharp knife, cut into 1-inch squares. Store in an airtight container between sheets of waxed paper or individually wrapped in waxed-paper squares. The caramels will keep at room temperature for up to 3 days, in the refrigerator for up to 2 weeks, or in the freezer for up to 2 months.

MAKES ABOUT 2 DOZEN CANDIES

family favorites

caramel nut corn

HONEY-LACED CARAMEL GLAZES POPCORN, ALMONDS, AND PECANS FOR AN ADDICTIVE SNACK TO PLEASE ALL AGES. PACKAGE THE SWEET CORN IN A BIG GIFT TIN WITH A BRIGHT SCARLET BOW FOR THE FAMILY NEXT DOOR. YOU CAN QUICKLY POP CORN IN A MICROWAVE OVEN USING PREPACKAGED CORN KERNELS SOLD SPECIFICALLY FOR MICROWAVE USE, OR POP YOUR OWN KERNELS IN A BIG POT ON THE STOVE TOP.

8 cups popped corn
$\frac{3}{4}$ cup toasted almonds (page 18)
$\frac{3}{4}$ cup toasted pecans (page 18)
$\frac{3}{4}$ cup sugar
$\frac{1}{4}$ cup light corn syrup
$\frac{1}{4}$ cup honey
$\frac{1}{4}$ cup water
$\frac{1}{8}$ teaspoon baking soda
2 tablespoons unsalted butter
$\frac{1}{2}$ cup half-and-half or evaporated milk

Preheat the oven to 120°F. Line a baking sheet with aluminum foil. Lightly oil the foil.

Put the popped corn and nuts in an oiled heat-proof bowl and place in the oven. In a heavy, 3-quart saucepan, combine the sugar, corn syrup, honey, and water and stir to blend. Place over medium heat and bring to a boil, stirring constantly. Add the baking soda and stir well. Insert a candy thermometer in the pan. Add the butter and half-and-half or evaporated milk and stir well. Cook over medium heat, stirring occasionally, until the temperature reaches 264°F.

If sugar crystals form on the pan sides, wash them down with a pastry brush dipped in warm water.

Immediately pour the hot caramel over the popped corn and nuts and toss with 2 forks to distribute evenly. Turn out onto the prepared baking sheet and use the forks to pull the mixture into bite-sized pieces. Let cool thoroughly.

Store in an airtight container at room temperature for up to 2 weeks.

MAKES ABOUT 10 CUPS

POPCORN BALLS: Omit the nuts. Pour the hot caramel over the popped corn and toss as directed. Let the corn cool just until it can be handled, then pick it up by the handful and shape into large balls. Wrap in waxed paper and twist ends. Makes about 12 balls.

M&M'S VARIATION: Substitute $1\frac{1}{2}$ cups M&M'S for the nuts.

pecan turtles

THE CREAMY, SOFT CARAMEL IS IDEAL FOR SEALING TOGETHER THE WHIMSICAL TURTLES FORMED BY A CLUSTER OF PECANS. THESE LOOK ENCHANTING DISPLAYED ON A PEDESTAL PLATE FOR A TEEN'S HOLIDAY PARTY.

$2\frac{1}{2}$ cups pecan halves (192 halves)
1 cup light corn syrup
1 cup sugar
$\frac{1}{4}$ cup water
Pinch of baking soda
$\frac{1}{4}$ cup unsalted butter
$\frac{3}{4}$ cup evaporated milk
8 ounces bittersweet chocolate, finely chopped, or 8 ounces (about $1\frac{1}{3}$ cups) semisweet chocolate chips
1 teaspoon vegetable oil

Line a baking sheet with aluminum foil and lightly oil the foil. Using 4 pecan halves per cluster, arrange the pecan halves on the prepared baking sheet to form about 48 clusters, spacing the clusters at least 1 inch apart.

In a heavy, 3-quart saucepan, combine the corn syrup, sugar, and water and stir to blend. Place over medium heat and bring to a boil, stirring constantly. Add the baking soda and stir well. Insert a candy thermometer in the pan. Add the butter and stir until incorporated. Add the evaporated milk while stirring constantly. Cook over medium heat, stirring occasionally, until the temperature reaches 242°F. If sugar crystals form on the pan sides, wash them down with a pastry brush dipped in warm water.

Remove from the heat and let the caramel stand until it cools to 200°F. Spoon 1 tablespoon of caramel into the center of each pecan cluster. Refrigerate the clusters until firm, about 15 minutes.

Put the chocolate and oil in the top of a double boiler over hot, not simmering, water, and melt, stirring constantly until smooth. Remove from the heat and let cool to 78° to 80°F. Pour the chocolate evenly over the caramel centers only. Refrigerate until firm.

Store in an airtight container between sheets of waxed paper at room temperature for up to 5 days or in the refrigerator for up to 2 weeks.

MAKES ABOUT 48 CANDIES

vinegar candy

VINEGAR WAS AN EARLY CANDY FLAVORING, PRECEDING THE USE OF VANILLA OR MINT. MANY OLDER NEW ENGLANDERS REMEMBER THIS CANDY AS AN IMPORTANT PART OF THEIR CHILDHOOD CHRISTMAS SEASONS. THE TAFFY WAS ORIGINALLY POPULARIZED BY SOPHIE MAY, AUTHOR OF THE "DOTTY DIMPLE" STORIES, PUBLISHED IN THE 1860S, PLUS DOZENS OF CHILDREN'S BOOKS. A RECIPE IN *THE AMERICAN HERITAGE COOKBOOK* CALLS THIS CANDY DOTTY DIMPLE'S VINEGAR CANDY.

2 cups sugar
$\frac{1}{2}$ cup cider vinegar
2 tablespoons unsalted butter

Oil a marble slab or a baking sheet.

In a heavy, 3-quart saucepan, combine the sugar, vinegar, and butter and stir well. Place over medium heat and bring to a boil, stirring constantly, until the sugar is dissolved. Cover and boil for 2 to 3 minutes. Uncover and insert a candy thermometer in the pan. Increase the heat to medium-high and cook, stirring occasionally, until the temperature reaches 260°F. If sugar crystals form on the pan sides, brush them down with a pastry brush dipped in warm water.

Turn the mixture onto the prepared work surface, and let cool until it is lukewarm and can be handled comfortably, 5 to 10 minutes. Butter your hands and pull the taffy with your fingertips until it is white, light, and porous, 10 to 15 minutes. Stretch it into a rope about 1 inch in diameter, and snip into 1-inch pieces with oiled scissors.

Pack the pieces between sheets of waxed paper in an airtight container. Store at room temperature for up to 2 weeks.

MAKES ABOUT 40 PIECES

family favorites

honey taffy

FROM THE LATE EIGHTEENTH CENTURY UNTIL WELL INTO THE TWENTIETH, TAFFY PULLS WERE A FAVORITE FORM OF ENTERTAINMENT FOR YOUNG PEOPLE DURING THE HOLIDAY SEASON. THE RECIPES WERE RARELY WRITTEN DOWN. CANDY SHOPS AT THE SEASHORE FEATURED SALTWATER TAFFY, SIMPLY MADE BY ADDING SALT TO THE RECIPE WHILE COOKING IT.

1 cup sugar
¼ cup water
⅓ cup honey or light corn syrup

Oil a marble slab or a baking sheet.

In a heavy, 2-quart saucepan, combine the sugar, water, and honey or corn syrup and stir to blend. Place over medium heat and bring to a boil, stirring constantly. Cover and boil for 2 to 3 minutes. Uncover and insert a candy thermometer in the pan. Increase the heat to medium-high and cook without stirring until the thermometer reaches 270°F. If sugar crystals form on the pan sides, brush them down with a pastry brush dipped in warm water.

Turn the mixture onto the prepared work surface, and let cool until it is lukewarm and can be handled comfortably, 5 to 10 minutes. Gather the taffy into a ball and pull with your fingertips until light and porous, 10 to 15 minutes. Stretch it into a rope about 1 inch in diameter, and snip into 1-inch pieces with oiled scissors.

Pack the pieces between sheets of waxed paper in an airtight container. Store at room temperature for up to 2 weeks.

MAKES ABOUT 24 PIECES

family favorites

chocolate-dipped fruit, page 88

fruit & nut confections

SUGARPLUMS | CHOCO-NUT CANDY BARS | DUO-CHOCOLATE PEPPERMINT BARK | CHOCOLATE NUT BARK | CHOCOLATE-DIPPED CANDIED ORANGE PEEL | APRICOT-ALMOND CHOCOLATE CLUSTERS | CANDIED CARDAMOM PISTACHIOS | CHOCOLATE-DIPPED FRUIT

sugarplums

EMBLEMATIC OF THE CHRISTMAS SEASON, THESE HEALTHFUL FRUIT-AND-NUT BALLS ARE A SNACKER'S DELIGHT ANY TIME OF DAY. THEY ARE ALSO THE CANDY MAKER'S FRIEND, NEEDING JUST A QUICK SPIN IN A FOOD PROCESSOR.

$1\frac{1}{3}$ cups pitted dates
$\frac{2}{3}$ cup dried apricots
1 cup almonds, toasted (page 18)
$\frac{1}{3}$ cup raw pistachios
$\frac{1}{3}$ cup candied ginger
2 tablespoons grated orange zest
About 2 tablespoons fresh lemon juice or brandy
Demerara sugar, turbinado sugar, or confectioners' sugar (optional)

Line a baking sheet with waxed paper.

Place the dates, apricots, nuts, ginger, and orange zest in a food processor and process until finely minced. Add just enough lemon juice or brandy to enable the mixture to stick together and process to blend.

Shape the mixture into 1-inch balls and roll in sugar to coat evenly, if desired. Place on the prepared baking sheet and let air-dry until no longer sticky, 1 to 2 hours.

To store, line an airtight container with waxed paper and layer the balls in it between sheets of waxed paper. Refrigerate for up to 2 weeks.

MAKES ABOUT 4 DOZEN CANDIES

choco-nut candy bars

DRIED AND CANDIED FRUITS AND TOASTED ALMONDS STREAK CHOCOLATE WAFERS FOR A DELECTABLE TASTE TREAT. THESE ARE IDEAL FOR WRAPPING IN FOIL AND TUCKING INTO CHRISTMAS STOCKINGS.

$\frac{1}{3}$ cup sweetened shredded dried coconut

$\frac{3}{4}$ cup almonds, coarsely chopped

8 ounces bittersweet chocolate, tempered (page 17) if desired

$\frac{1}{2}$ cup dried apricots, cut into slivers

$\frac{1}{4}$ cup chopped candied ginger or whole golden raisins

$\frac{1}{4}$ cup chopped candied orange peel (optional)

Preheat the oven to 350°F. Scatter the coconut in one baking pan and the almonds in another pan. Place in the oven until the coconut and the nuts are lightly toasted, about 5 minutes for the coconut and 8 to 10 minutes for the nuts, stirring once or twice. Remove from the oven and pour onto separate small plates to cool.

Line an 8-inch baking square pan with aluminum foil, extending it up the sides. Lightly oil the foil. Melt the chocolate in the top of a double boiler over hot, not simmering, water, stirring constantly until smooth.

In a bowl, combine the toasted almonds, apricots, ginger or raisins, half the coconut, and the candied orange peel, if desired, and toss to distribute evenly. Pour this mixture into the chocolate and stir to coat evenly. Turn the chocolate mixture into the prepared pan and, using a flexible metal spatula, spread until smooth. Sprinkle the top evenly with the remaining coconut. Refrigerate until set, about 45 minutes.

Remove the pan from the refrigerator and, using the foil, lift the candy from the pan. Peel away the foil. Cut into 1-inch-wide strips, then cut across the width to make 1-by-2-inch bars.

Line an airtight tin with foil and place the bars in the tin. Store in the refrigerator for up to 1 month. The bars taste best at room temperature.

MAKES 32 BARS

duo-chocolate peppermint bark

PINK-AND-WHITE PEPPERMINT CANDY TOPS LAYERS OF DARK AND WHITE CHOCOLATE FOR THIS DAZZLING CONFECTION. SERVE ON A TRAY WITH CHRISTMAS COOKIES FOR A TEATIME TREAT.

6 ounces bittersweet chocolate, chopped, or
   6 ounces (about 1 cup) semisweet chocolate chips
2 teaspoons vegetable oil
6 ounces (about 1 cup) white chocolate chips
½ cup crushed peppermint candy

Line a 9-inch square baking pan with aluminum foil, extending it up the pan sides. Combine the bitter-sweet chocolate or semisweet chips with 1 teaspoon of the oil in the top of a double boiler and melt over hot, not simmering, water, stirring constantly until smooth.

Immediately pour the chocolate into the pre-pared pan and tilt the pan or tap on the countertop once or twice to spread the chocolate evenly. Refrig-erate until set, about 30 minutes. Rinse the top of the double boiler.

Melt the white chocolate chips with the remain-ing 1 teaspoon oil in the top of the double boiler over hot, not simmering, water, stirring constantly until smooth. Immediately pour over the dark chocolate layer and tilt the pan or tap on the countertop once or twice to spread the chocolate evenly. Scatter the peppermint candy evenly over the surface. Refrigerate until set, about 30 minutes.

Remove the pan from the refrigerator and, using the foil, lift the candy from the pan. Peel away the foil. Break the candy into small pieces. Store in an airtight container at room temperature for up to 5 days or in the refrigerator for up to 2 weeks.

MAKES ABOUT 30 PIECES

chocolate nut bark

PERSONALIZE THIS CANDY WITH YOUR FAVORITE NUT. CHOCOLATE BARK TRAVELS WELL. LEAVE THE BAR WHOLE, WRAP IT IN FOIL, AND PACK IT IN A HEAVY-DUTY CORRUGATED GIFT BOX FOR SAFE DELIVERY.

12 ounces bittersweet chocolate, chopped, or
    12 ounces (about 2 cups) semisweet
    chocolate chips
2 teaspoons vegetable oil
1 cup coarsely chopped Brazil nuts, macadamia
    nuts, or toasted almonds (page 18)

Line a 9-inch baking pan with aluminum foil, extending it up the pan sides. Melt the chocolate with the oil in the top of a double boiler over hot, not simmering, water, stirring constantly until smooth. Stir in the nuts, coating thoroughly.

Immediately pour the chocolate into the prepared pan and tilt the pan or tap on the counter once or twice to spread the chocolate evenly. Refrigerate until set, about 30 minutes.

Remove the pan from the refrigerator and, using the foil, lift the candy from the pan. Peel away the foil. Break the candy into small pieces. Store in an airtight container at room temperature for up to 5 days or in the refrigerator for up to 2 weeks.

MAKES ABOUT 30 PIECES

chocolate-dipped candied orange peel

IT IS EASY TO CANDY ORANGE PEEL AT HOME, AND THE TASTE IS SUPERIOR TO COMMERCIAL PRODUCTS. YOU CAN CUT THE TANGY FRUIT PEEL INTO TRIANGLES, AND CLOAK THE TIPS WITH CHOCOLATE FOR A TART-SWEET TREAT. YOU CAN ALSO LEAVE THE CANDIED PEEL PLAIN FOR USE IN MANY HOLIDAY CANDY AND DESSERT RECIPES. IT IS IDEAL FOR GARNISHING TRUFFLES AND MARZIPAN LOGS.

4 oranges

$1\frac{1}{3}$ cups sugar

$1\frac{1}{3}$ cups water

6 ounces bittersweet chocolate, chopped, or 6 ounces (about 1 cup) semisweet chocolate chips

Remove the peel from each orange in 4 uniform pieces. Reserve the fruits for another use. Place the peels in a saucepan, add water to cover, and bring to a boil over medium-high heat. Boil for 1 minute, then pour off the water. Add water to cover again, bring to a boil, and boil for 1 minute, then again pour off the water.

Using a tablespoon, scrape off as much of the white pith from the orange peel as possible. Cut the peel into triangles about 1 inch long and $\frac{1}{2}$ inch across at the base. Combine the sugar and $1\frac{1}{3}$ cups water in a saucepan and bring to a boil over medium-high heat, stirring to dissolve the sugar. Add the orange triangles to the syrup and boil, uncovered, until the syrup is fully absorbed, 15 to 20 minutes.

When the orange peel is ready, lay the triangles on a sheet of waxed paper and let dry about 1 hour. (If you do not intend to chocolate-dip them, place them in an airtight container and refrigerate for up to 2 weeks or freeze for up to 4 months.)

Meanwhile, melt the chocolate in the top of a double boiler over hot, not simmering, water, stirring constantly until smooth. Using a small flexible metal spatula, spread the chocolate over the tip of each orange triangle, coating both sides. As they are coated, lay them on a sheet of aluminum foil. Let cool at room temperature until firm, about 1 hour.

Store in an airtight container in the refrigerator for up to 2 weeks or in the freezer for up to 4 months.

MAKES ABOUT 6 DOZEN PIECES

apricot-almond chocolate clusters

THESE IMPRESSIVE CANDIES ARE ULTRAFAST TO PREPARE AND ALLOW FOR MYRIAD FLAVOR VARIA-
TIONS. MAKE AN ASSORTMENT (SEE VARIATIONS), WRAP THEM INDIVIDUALLY, AND PUT THEM IN A
GLASS BOWL WITH A FEW SHINY ORNAMENTS FOR DECOR AND AS A FINALE TO A HOLIDAY FEAST.

6 ounces (about 1 cup) semisweet chocolate
   chips
1 teaspoon vegetable oil
$\frac{1}{2}$ cup diced dried apricots
$\frac{1}{2}$ cup almonds, toasted (page 18) and coarsely
   chopped

Line a baking sheet with waxed paper. Melt the
chocolate chips with the oil in the top of a double
boiler over hot, not simmering, water, stirring constantly until smooth. Remove from the heat and stir
in the apricots and nuts.

Using a 1-inch scoop or melon baller, form the
chocolate mixture into balls and drop onto the prepared baking sheet. Refrigerate until set, about
15 minutes.

Store in an airtight container in the refrigerator
for up to 1 month or in the refrigerator for up to
2 months. Bring to room temperature before serving.

MAKES ABOUT 16 CANDIES

VARIATIONS:

HAZELNUT-CHERRY CHOCOLATE CLUSTERS:
Substitute $\frac{1}{2}$ cup dried cherries and $\frac{1}{2}$ cup hazelnuts, toasted and skinned (page 18), then coarsely
chopped, for the apricots and almonds.

GRANOLA-PISTACHIO MILK CHOCOLATE CLUSTERS:
Substitute milk chocolate chips for the semisweet
chocolate chips. Substitute $\frac{1}{2}$ cup granola and
$\frac{1}{2}$ cup roasted pistachios, coarsely chopped, for the
apricots and almonds.

CANDIED ORANGE–HAZELNUT CHOCOLATE
CLUSTERS: Substitute $\frac{1}{3}$ cup minced candied
orange peel and $\frac{1}{2}$ cup hazelnuts, toasted and
skinned (page 18), then coarsely chopped, for the
apricots and almonds.

CANDIED GINGER–MACADAMIA CHOCOLATE
CLUSTERS: Substitute $\frac{1}{3}$ cup minced candied ginger and $\frac{2}{3}$ cup coarsely chopped macadamia nuts
for the apricots and almonds.

fruit & nut
confections

candied cardamom pistachios

AN ASSORTMENT OF THESE SPICED NUTS MAKES A HANDSOME HOLIDAY GIFT PACKAGE. WITH A SPICY, SWEET CRUNCH, THE NUTS ARE AN ADDICTIVE, VERSATILE TREAT AS A CANDY OR FOR SNACKING. THEY ARE ALSO SUPERB SCATTERED OVER VANILLA BEAN ICE CREAM OR A CHOCOLATE SUNDAE OR CAKE.

1 tablespoon honey

1 tablespoon sugar

$\frac{1}{2}$ teaspoon ground cardamom

1 tablespoon water

1 cup raw pistachios

Preheat the oven to 350°F. Line a baking sheet with aluminum foil, and lightly oil the foil.

In a heavy, 1- or $1\frac{1}{2}$-quart saucepan, combine the honey, sugar, cardamom, and water and stir to blend. Bring to a boil over medium-high heat, add the nuts, and boil for 2 minutes, shaking the pan to coat the nuts. Turn the nuts onto the prepared baking sheet, spreading them into a single layer as much as possible.

Bake until golden brown, 8 to 10 minutes. Remove from the oven and let cool. Using your fingers, separate the nuts. Store in an airtight container at room temperature for up to 1 week, in the refrigerator for up to 1 month, or in the freezer for up to 2 months.

MAKES 1 CUP

VARIATIONS:

Substitute any one of the following combinations for the cardamom and pistachios:

$\frac{1}{2}$ teaspoon ground cinnamon
and 1 cup walnut halves

$\frac{1}{2}$ teaspoon ground allspice
and 1 cup almonds

$\frac{1}{2}$ teaspoon ground ginger
and 1 cup pecan halves

$\frac{1}{8}$ teaspoon freshly grated nutmeg
and 1 cup skinned, toasted hazelnuts (page 18)

chocolate-dipped fruit

BECAUSE OF THEIR CHOCOLATE CLOAKS, THESE FRUITS ARE CLASSED AS CONFECTIONS. A TRAY OF THEM MAKES A STUNNING DESSERT ON A HOLIDAY BUFFET TABLE, WITH THE BITE-SIZED MORSELS A WELCOME JUICY CONTRAST TO OTHER SWEETS AND PASTRIES. THEY ALSO OFTEN APPEAR PAIRED WITH TRUFFLES ON TRAYS OF FRENCH SWEETS.

8 ounces bittersweet chocolate, chopped, or 8 ounces (about $1\frac{1}{3}$ cup) semisweet chocolate chips

$\frac{1}{4}$ cup orange-flavored liqueur such as Grand Marnier or Cointreau or strong brewed coffee

Choice of 5 cups strawberries with stems; 8 tangerines, peeled and sectioned; or 1 pound dried apricots or dried pears, cut into wedges; 5 kiwi fruits, peeled and sliced lengthwise

MAKES ABOUT 20 SERVINGS (2 OR 3 PIECES PER PERSON)

VARIATIONS: White chocolate chips may be substituted for the dark chocolate. Omit the coffee for flavoring. Candied ginger slices or marshmallows may also be chocolate-dipped.

Melt the chocolate with the liqueur or coffee in the top of a double boiler over hot, not simmering, water, stirring constantly until smooth.

Line a baking sheet with aluminum foil. Dip the fruit pieces halfway into the chocolate and place on the prepared baking sheet. If using berries, place stem-ends down. Refrigerate until the chocolate sets, about 15 minutes.

Serve immediately, or refrigerate for up to 3 hours. Remove from the refrigerator 15 minutes before serving.

sources

index

table of equivalents

sources

Cost Plus Imports
Retail stores nationwide
Tel: 800-COST-PLUS
www.costplus.com
Specialty bags and wrappers

Crate and Barrel
Retail stores nationwide
Tel: 900-967-6696
www.crateandbarrel.com
Catalog/mail order
Specialty cookware

Dean & DeLuca
Retail stores nationwide
Tel: 212-431-1691; outside New York: 800-826-9243
www.deandeluca.com
Catalog/mail order
Cookware and specialty ingredients

Eaton's Cake and Candy Supply Store
Route 28 bypass
114 Londonberry Turnpike
Hooksett, NH 03106
Tel: 800-545-7420
www.nhwedding.com/eatonschocolate/
Order by phone
Classes, chocolate parties

Gloria's Cake and Candy Supplies
3755 Sawtell Boulevard
West Los Angeles, CA 90066
Tel: 310-391-4557
www.gloriascakecandysuplys.com
Specialty ingredients

Kitchen Krafts
P.O. Box 442
Waukon, IA 52172
Tel: 800-776-0575
www.kitchenkrafts.com
Catalog/mail order
Chocolate, candy-making supplies

Penzeys Ltd. Spice House
P.O. Box 1448
Waukesha, WI 53187
Tel: 800-741-7787
www.penzeys.com
Catalog/mail order
Spices

G. B. Ratto & Company
821 Washington Street
Oakland, CA 94607
Tel: 800-325-3483
Catalog/mail order
Chocolate

Scharffen Berger Chocolate Maker
914 Heinz Avenue
Berkeley, CA 94710
Tel: 510-981-4066
www.scharffenberger.com
Mail order
Chocolate, cocoa, tours

Sur La Table
Retail stores nationwide
Tel: 800-243-0852
www.surlatable.com
Catalog/mail order
Cookware

Sweet Celebrations
P.O. Box 39426
Edina, MN 55439
Tel: 800-328-6722
www.sweetc.com
Catalog/mail order
Chocolate, candy-making supplies

The Chocolate Box
321 Balsam Street
Grants, NM 87020
Tel: 505-285-6601
www.tcb@tcbsupply.com
Catalog/mail order
Candy-making foil, chocolate, wooden sucker sticks

Trader Joe's
Retail stores nationwide
Tel: 800-SHOP-TJS
www.traderjoes.com
Bar chocolate, dried fruits, shelled pistachios, other nuts

Vanilla Company
P.O. Box 3206
Santa Cruz, CA 95063
Tel: 800-757-7511
www.vanilla.com
Mail order
Various types of vanilla

Willams-Sonoma
Retail stores nationwide
Tel: 800-541-1262
www.williams-sonoma.com
Catalog/mail order
Cookware

Zabar's
Tel: 212-496-1234; outside New York: 800-697-6301
www.zabars.com
Catalog/mail order
Chocolate, candy ingredients, cookware

index

almond paste, 32

Apricot-Almond Chocolate Clusters, 85

brittle

    Macadamia Chocolate Crunch, 35

    Peanut Brittle, 36

Candied Cardamom Pistachios, 86

Candied Cinnamon Walnuts, 86

Candied Ginger-Macadamia Chocolate Clusters, 85

Candied Ginger-Pecans, 86

Cappuccino-Walnut Fudge Balls, 62

caramel, 20

    Chocolate Caramels, 67

    Chocolate-Coated Pecan Caramels, 60

    Coffee-Walnut Caramels, 66

    Maple Pecan Caramels, 63

Caramel Nut Corn, 68

chocolate, 10–11, 16–17

    Apricot-Almond Chocolate Clusters, 85

    Chocolate Caramels, 67

    Chocolate-Coated Pecan Caramels, 60

    Chocolate-Dipped Candied Orange Peel, 83

    Chocolate-Dipped Fruit, 88

    Chocolate Marzipan Logs, 39

    Chocolate Nut Bark, 82

    Chocolate Panforte, 26

    Choco-Nut Candy Bars, 79

    Classic Chocolate Truffles, 44

    Cognac-Goat Cheese Truffles, 48

    Duo-Chocolate Peppermint Bark, 80

    Eggnog Truffles, 49

    English Toffee, 25

    Hazelnut Praline Truffles, 45

    Macadamia Chocolate Crunch, 35

    Macadamia-Ginger White Chocolate Truffles, 55

    Mocha Chocolate Truffles, 53

    Old-Fashioned Fudge, 58

    Orange Liqueur Chocolate Truffles, 47

    Pecan Turtles, 70

    Peppermint Candy Truffles, 42

    Pistachio-Cherry White Chocolate Truffles, 50

    Raspberry Chocolate Truffles, 52

Chocolate Caramels, 67

Chocolate-Coated Pecan Caramels, 60

Candied Orange Peel, 83

Chocolate-Dipped Fruit, 88

Chocolate Marzipan Logs, 39

Chocolate Nut Bark, 82

Chocolate Panforte, 26

Choco-Nut Candy Bars, 79

Christmastime Marzipan, 32–33

cinnamon, 11

    Candied Cinnamon Walnuts, 86

    Chocolate Panforte, 26

    Lollipops, 65

    Panforte of Siena, 24

Classic Chocolate Truffles, 44

coffee, 11

    Cappuccino-Walnut Fudge Balls, 62

    Coffee-Walnut Caramels, 66

    Mocha Chocolate Truffles, 53

Coffee-Walnut Caramels, 66

Cognac-Goat Cheese Truffles, 48

Duo-Chocolate Peppermint Bark, 80

Eggnog Truffles, 49

English Toffee, 25

equipment

    candy thermometer, 13

    cooling pans, 13

    electric mixer, 14

    food processor, 14

    knives, 14

    marble slab, 14

    saucepans, 14

    small tools, 14–15

    storage containers, 15

French Almond Nougat, 31

fruit

    Apricot-Almond Chocolate Clusters, 85

    Chocolate-Dipped Candied Orange Peel, 83

    Chocolate-Dipped Fruit, 88

    Chocolate Marzipan Logs, 39

    Chocolate Panforte, 26

    Choco-Nut Candy Bars, 79

    Christmastime Marzipan, 32–33

    Holiday Divinity, 38

    Orange Liqueur Chocolate Truffles, 47

    Panforte of Siena, 24

    Pistachio-Cherry White Chocolate Truffles, 50

    Raspberry Chocolate Truffles, 52

    Sugarplums, 76

    Torrone, 28–29

fudge

    Cappuccino-Walnut Fudge Balls, 62

    Old-Fashioned Fudge, 58

    Peanut Butter Fudge, 59

ginger

    Candied Ginger-Macadamia Chocolate Clusters, 85

    Candied Ginger-Pecans, 86

    Chocolate-Dipped Fruit, 88

    Chocolate Panforte, 26

    Choco-Nut Candy Bars, 79

    Macadamia-Ginger White Chocolate Truffles, 55

    Panforte of Siena, 24

    Sugarplums, 76

hard candy, 11

    Lollipops, 65

    Vinegar Candy, 71

Hazelnut Praline Truffles, 45

history of Christmas candies, 9

Holiday Divinity, 38

Honey Taffy, 73

ingredients, about

    butter, 10

    chocolate, 10–11

    cream, 11

    flavorings, 11

    nuts, 11

    oil, 11

    sweeteners, 12

liquor, liqueur, 11

    Chocolate-Dipped Fruit, 88

    Chocolate Marzipan Logs, 39

    Classic Chocolate Truffles, 44

    Cognac-Goat Cheese Truffles, 48

    Eggnog Truffles, 49

    Hazelnut Praline Truffles, 45

    Macadamia-Ginger White Chocolate Truffles, 55

    Orange Liqueur Chocolate Truffles, 47

    Peppermint Candy Truffles, 42

    Pistachio-Cherry White Chocolate Truffles, 50

    Raspberry Chocolate Truffles, 52

    Sugarplums, 76

Lollipops, 65

Macadamia Chocolate Crunch, 35

Macadamia-Ginger White Chocolate Truffles, 55

Maple Pecan Caramels, 63

marzipan, 32

    Chocolate Marzipan Logs, 39

    Christmastime Marzipan, 32–33

Mocha Chocolate Truffles, 53

nuts, 11, 18

    Apricot-Almond Chocolate Clusters, 85

    Candied Cardamom Pistachios, 86

    Cappuccino-Walnut Fudge Balls, 62

    Caramel Nut Corn, 68

    Chocolate Caramels, 67

    Chocolate-Coated Pecan Caramels, 60

    Chocolate Marzipan Logs, 39

    Chocolate Nut Bark, 82

    Choco-Nut Candy Bars, 79

    Christmastime Marzipan, 32–33

    Coffee-Walnut Caramels, 66

    Duo-Chocolate Peppermint Bark, 80

    English Toffee, 25

    French Almond Nougat, 31

    Hazelnut Praline Truffles, 45

    Holiday Divinity, 38

    Macadamia Chocolate Crunch, 35

    Macadamia-Ginger White Chocolate Truffles, 55

    Maple Pecan Caramels, 63

    Old-Fashioned Fudge, 58

    Panforte of Siena, 24

    Peanut Brittle, 36

    Peanut Butter Fudge, 59

    Pecan Pralines, 34

Pecan Turtles, 70
Pistachio-Cherry White Chocolate Truffles, 50
Sugarplums, 76
Torrone, 28-29

Old-Fashioned Fudge, 58
Orange Liqueur Chocolate Truffles, 47

Panforte of Siena, 24
Peanut Brittle, 36
Peanut Butter Fudge, 59
Pecan Pralines, 34
Pecan Turtles, 70
Peppermint Candy Truffles, 42
Pistachio-Cherry White Chocolate Truffles, 50
Popcorn Balls, 68

Raspberry Chocolate Truffles, 52

Sugarplums, 76

techniques
blanching nuts, 18
chopping chocolate, 16
chopping nuts, 18
grating chocolate, 16
grinding nuts, 18
nougat, 17–18
melting chocolate, 16
packaging candies, 21

sugaring prevention, 19
syrup stages, 19–20
tempering chocolate, 17
toasting nuts, 18
troubleshooting, 20

Torrone, 28–29
truffles
Classic Chocolate Truffles, 44
Cognac-Goat Cheese Truffles, 48
Eggnog Truffles, 49
Hazelnut Praline Truffles, 45
Macadamia-Ginger White Chocolate Truffles, 55
Mocha Chocolate Truffles, 53
Orange Liqueur Chocolate Truffles, 47
Peppermint Candy Truffles, 42
Pistachio-Cherry White Chocolate Truffles, 50
Raspberry Chocolate Truffles, 52

vanilla extract, 11
Cappuccino-Walnut Fudge Balls, 62
Chocolate Caramels, 67
Chocolate-Coated Pecan Caramels, 60
French Almond Nougat, 31
Holliday Divinity, 38
Macadamia Chocolate Crunch, 35
Maple Pecan Caramels, 63
Old-Fashioned Fudge, 58
Peanut Brittle, 36
Peanut Butter Fudge, 59
Vinegar Candy, 71

table of equivalents

THE EXACT EQUIVALENTS IN THE FOLLOWING TABLES HAVE BEEN ROUNDED FOR CONVENIENCE.

LIQUID / DRY MEASURES
U.S. TO METRIC

¼ teaspoon = 1.25 milliliters

½ teaspoon = 2.5 milliliters

1 teaspoon = 5 milliliters

1 tablespoon (3 teaspoons) = 15 milliliters

1 fluid ounce (2 tablespoons) = 30 milliliters

¼ cup = 60 milliliters

⅓ cup = 80 milliliters

½ cup = 120 milliliters

1 cup = 240 milliliters

1 pint (2 cups) = 480 milliliters

1 quart (4 cups, 32 ounces) = 960 milliliters

1 gallon (4 quarts) = 3.84 liters

1 ounce (by weight) = 28 grams

1 pound = 454 grams

2.2 pounds = 1 kilogram

OVEN TEMPERATURE

FAHRENHEIT	GAS	CELSIUS
250	½	120
275	1	140
300	2	150
325	3	160
350	4	180
375	5	190
400	6	200
425	7	220
450	8	230
475	9	240
500	10	260

LENGTH
U.S. TO METRIC

⅛ inch = 3 millimeters

¼ inch = 6 millimeters

½ inch = 12 millimeters

1 inch = 2.5 centimeters